The Complete Book of Gingerbread

The Complete Book of Gingerbread

VALERIE BARRETT

THE
APPLE
PRESS

A QUINTET BOOK

Published by The Apple Press
6 Blundell Street
London N7 9BH

ISBN 1-85076-375-5

This book was designed and produced by
Quintet Publishing Limited
6 Blundell Street
London N7 9BH

Project Editor: Laura Sandelson
Creative Director: Richard Dewing
Designers: Stuart Walden, Ian Hunt
Photographer: Trevor Wood

Typeset in Great Britain by
Central Southern Typesetters, Eastbourne
Manufactured in Hong Kong by
Regent Publishing Services Limited
Printed in Hong Kong by
Leefung-Asco Printers Limited

Contents

Introduction

GINGER: A MOST ANCIENT ROOT

All ginger comes from a strange twisted root or rhizome called *zingiber officinale*. The reed-like plant itself has long leaves and a yellow and purple flower that rather resembles an iris. The fat creeping root is sometimes known as the "hand" as it can look like a fat hand with strange fingers. This root is the hot, pungent spice – ginger – that has been known from ancient times.

Ginger has its origins in the moist tropical jungles of South East Asia. It was first used in China and India; by Roman times, dried ginger was being used in the Middle East and Southern Europe. The Romans used ginger for cooking and medicinal purposes and, as the Empire grew, so did the demand for spices. In the 2nd Century AD, caravans regularly travelled from China, loaded with silk, ginger and cinnamon, to a meeting point in Central Asia. Here the Romans bartered for these luxuries with glass, pottery, beads and wine.

As Europe expanded, the trade routes became more numerous. Ginger, pepper and cinnamon were much sought after, presented as gifts to kings and church dignitaries or sometimes used as trade fees. A pound of ginger held the same value as a sheep.

Ginger and other spices became very popular in all types of cooking. One of the earliest known cookery books of modern Europe was *Le Viandier de Taillevent* by Guillaume Tirel. Compiled in 1375, Tirel was cook to Charles V of France. He gives the following recipe for a condiment known as *cameline*:

"Pound ginger, plenty of cinnamon, cloves, cardomom, mace, long pepper if you wish, then squeeze out bread soaked in vinegar and strain them all together and salt it just right."

During the 15th century, the exploitation of the spice trade became very competitive. A

long chain of "middle men" had evolved, all making large profits. Anyone who could by-pass the usual trade routes by sailing direct to the Far East and the Spice Islands would, of course, make more profit themselves. There were major difficulties; ship design had to improve to cope with longer journeys and unknown seas had to be explored and maps charted. Circumnavigators, such as Columbus and Vasco de Gama, set off to find new lands and new sources of spices and foods. The Portuguese, Dutch and later English, French, Danes and Austrians set up trading companies to bring foods from the New World and later, from Asia and Africa, to Europe. The traffic

ABOVE Ginger roots being sorted for purchase. Today ginger is grown commercially all over the tropics, South China, Japan, The Caribbean, Queensland, West Africa, India and Indonesia.

of foodstuffs was by no means one way. Fruits, vegetables, grains and meats from Europe and Asia were carried to the New Worlds of America, Bahamas, Brazil and the Caribbean. The ginger rhizome was a particular example. Since it keeps alive for some time, the Spanish took them in sailing ships to the West Indies where they were transplanted and quickly became established.

TYPES OF GINGER

FRESH GINGER

"Fresh" is something of a misnomer as even the newly-harvested root is dried slightly in the sun before packing for sale. The greener it is, the less it has been dried. Very green ginger is hard to obtain and does not keep long.

The "hand" should be plump, firm and not too fibrous. The taste is mild and less "spicy" or "hot" than that of the ground spice. For use, fresh ginger is peeled, then chopped and grated or ground to a pulp before being used, mainly in savoury dishes such as curry. It also can be used in sweet dishes (see Ginger Rub-Up Cake), and indeed in tropical countries is preferred to the dried spice for most cooking. The root may be pickled in vinegar, canned, crystalized or preserved in syrup. The latter is called "stem" ginger and is from the young shoots with few fibres.

DRIED GINGER

This is the unskinned rhizome which is washed and dried in the sun. The classic way to use dried ginger is by "bruising" – that is, by hitting with a rolling pin to let the flavour escape. Dried ginger is usually known as root ginger.

POWDER OR GROUND GINGER

This is ground from the ginger root. It is used in sweet preparations such as breads, biscuits, cakes, puddings, sauces, ginger beer and wine, pickles, chutneys and in some meat, fish and ham dishes. It is best to buy small amounts of good quality ground ginger, as the volatile essential oil responsible for the flavour is easily lost in the air.

THE HISTORY OF GINGERBREAD

The gingerbread tradition really began in Europe and is inextricably entwined with honey cake. It was the Germans, Austrians and Hungarians who developed a honey and spice flour-based dough, sometimes enriched with the addition of candied fruit or nuts. In France a simpler recipe, similar to bread but flavoured with honey and spice, became known as *Pain d'epice.*

CONTINENTAL GINGERBREADS

In the many monasteries of Germany and Austria in the 11th century, there was plenty

BELOW A few of the many tasty gingerbread recipes featured in this book. From top: Grantham Gingerbread, Cornish Fairings, Gingernuts and Ginger Rich Flapjacks.

ABOVE Gingerbread molds can be true works of art, ranging from intricate designs which can be hung on a wall, to simple but bold. In this picture the heart, girl and sheep are modern American clay molds and in the center is a 19th-century wooden Dutch mold.

RIGHT The Gingerbread House was inspired by the story of Hansel and Gretel; the two children who came upon a house made of cake and could not resist the temptation. Today, Gingerbread Houses can be made in many variations for different occasions.

of "home-grown" honey. A sizeable portion was used to make "Lebkuchen" (gingerbread) which became very popular. The unique position of Nuremberg – geographically in the middle of Europe and at the heart of the Holy Roman Empire – made it the principal junction of the trade routes. Nuremberg merchants dealt in so many spices that they became known as "peppersacks." The bakers of honey-spice cakes were called "Lebzelter," and soon they were using most of the available spices in their recipes. These were bought by visitors and exported further afield. Nuremberg became renown as the "gingerbread capital" of the world. As with any major trading center, many fine craftsmen were attracted to the town. Sculptors, painters, woodcarvers and goldsmiths all contributed to the most beautiful gingerbread cakes in Europe. Gifted craftsmen carved intricate wooden molds, artists assisted with decoration in frosting or gold paint. Incredibly fancy hearts, angels, wreaths and other festive shapes were sold at fairs, carnivals and markets.

The flat honey and spice cakes sold in bundles of gray wrapping at fairs were known as "zelten." For religious holidays there were cakes in the image of saints, among them St. Nicholas. Sentimental gifts of gingerbread were bestowed at weddings, baptisms and birthdays, decorated with piped-on names, wise sayings and little homilies.

Eventually each town in German-speaking lands had its own variation of gingerbread, though, in fact, some did not even contain ginger. Thus these cakes are more often called honey, or spice cakes. In addition to Nuremberg's Lebkuchen, Basel had "Leckerli," Thorn had "Katharinchen," Aachen was famed for "Printen," Breslau produced "Bomben," Cologne was known for "Pfefferbrot" and the Rhineland had "Spekulatius." These variations resulted in strong competition and rivalry and there was even a so-called 200-year-old "Lebkuchen War." This was finally settled in 1927, when it was ruled that Nuremberger Lebkuchen might only be called so if made in the town itself. It became a copyright in much the same way as Champagne in France.

When pedlars sold gingerbread at fairs in England during the 17th century, it was nothing like the gingerbread of today. It was made from stale bread, honey, pepper, aniseed – with saffron or liqorice for coloring – and ginger. All this was mashed together, molded or shaped, and dried until hard and brittle. In 1609, Sir Hugh Plat, in his "Delights for Ladies," offered this recipe:

"To make Gingerbread. Take 3 stale Manchets, and grate them: drie them, and sift them thorow a fine sieve: then adde unto them one ounce of ginger, beeing beaten, and much Cinamon, one ounce of Liquorice and Anniseedes being beaten together, and searced, half a pound of sugar, then boile all these together in a posnet, with a quart of claret wine, til they come to a stiffe past with often stirring of it; and when it is stiffe, mold it on a table and so drive it thin, and print it in your moldes: dust your moldes with Cinamon, Ginger and Liquorice, beeing mixed together in fine powder. This is your Gingerbread used at the Court, and in all Gentlemens houses at festival times. It is otherwise called drie leach."

In England gingerbread was baked for holidays, saints' days, market days and annual fairs all over England. Sometimes little cookies called "fair buttons" or "fairings" were sold, 20 for a penny. At the great Goose Fair in Nottingham, little cones and tubes of gingerbread – Brandy Snaps – were sold, and at Ashbourne Fair in Derbyshire each August, it was traditional to have gingerbread sticks that were similar to shortbread. The pedlars and gingerbread sellers all had their special cry – "Gingerbread, very good bread, comfortable bread" – "Hot spiced gingerbread, smoking hot!."

After treacle (molasses) was introduced to England in the 17th century, recipes slowly began to change. Molasses replaced honey,

flour replaced bread, and eggs were used. Gingerbread also began to take several forms: it could be rolled out or in cookie, sponge, or cake form. Many local variations developed. In the North of England and Scotland, oatmeal was cheaper than flour and was used to make a type of gingerbread called "Parkin," "Perkin" or "Parken." In the North, parkin is sponge-like, but in Scotland it is a gingerbread cookie made with oatmeal. Beer was sometimes used instead of milk for mixing, and black molasses always replaced the sugar.

As people began to eat and cook more gingerbread and cake in their homes, the gingerbread seller slowly began to fade from the scene. However, in London streets,

ABOVE The gingerbread seller was a popular figure on the streets of 17th-century England. The gingerbread they sold was of a course texture and not as sweet as it is today.

gingernuts and breads, made by Jewish pastry cooks in Whitechapel, were sold by traders or "costermongers" up until the inter-war period. They sold them along with muffins, crumpets and Chelsea buns, and the cry had now become, "Here comes the Muffin Man!". In many ways the traditional European Lebzelter art perished. Nevertheless, gingerbread is still considered a European Christmas speciality. The gingerbread is decorated and hung on a tree, or made into houses covered in biscuits and sweets.

TRANSATLANTIC VARIATIONS

Gingerbread had made its way to America with the first early English settlers. They began baking the bread and cakes they used to have at home but with one crucial difference; they used maple syrup instead of sugar. The original simple English gingerbread recipes became adapted, transformed and re-invented as the population of New England grew to absorb other races such as Irish, Italian and Portuguese.

Regional variations began occurring as more people arrived. In Pennsylvania, the influence of German cooking was great and many traditional German gingerbreads reappeared in this area, especially at Christmas time. Even today, Pennsylvania has an enduring and distinctive style of baking, and around Christmas time an orgy of gingerbread and biscuit-baking takes place.

The North and Midwest of America welcomed the Northern and Middle Europeans. At Christmas it is still very common in the Midwest to have Scandinavian cookies like Pepparkaker (see page 33) or Lebkuchen (see page 35). Often one can find wives holding "coffee kolaches" (coffee mornings) at which European ginger cakes still reign. Many of the Austrian immigrants to the Midwest opened pastry shops, no doubt selling a variety of gingerbreads and cakes.

In the 18th century, some of the Anglo-Saxons moved to the South from their Eastern settlements. New immigrants to the South also swarmed from France, Spain and Canada (Arcadians of French descent). The original Indians and the Blacks brought in as slaves all contributed to a lively and enthusiastic cuisine. Ingredients obtainable in the South were different again, and buttermilk, cane syrup and even rum began to appear in gingerbread recipes. One well-known Southern ginger-cake is *Gateau Sirop* (*see* Louisiana Syrup Cake). Southern folk still do a lot of baking and neighbourliness is often expressed by the gift of a cake or batch of spicy cookies.

After 1880 the picture changed yet again, and immigrants flooded in to the USA from Southern, Central and Eastern Europe. They introduced new concepts of eating and cooking. This time they could bring more with them and they did not have to endure the physical hardships of the first settlers. They may well have brought some of their own cooking equipment – moulds, cutters, carved rolling pins. Some were very determined to keep their old customs and traditions, and so an extraordinary culinary patchwork evolved. Some old gingerbread recipes that had virtually disappeared in Europe have been preserved in America, and other totally new versions were created and are now truly indigenous. One prime example is Houston gingerbread.

Nowhere in the world is there a greater repertoire of gingerbread recipes than in America – there are so many variations in taste, form and presentation. At Christmas-time, gingerbread-making in America is in a class of its own – nowhere is such an array of "Susseback" (sweet bakings) made. With the rich choice of ingredients, baking aids, and decorative items, it is no wonder that the most spectacular gingerbread houses, boxes, nativity scenes, and Christmas centrepieces can be created by enthusiastic cooks.

RIGHT In Basel, Switzerland, special cakes are baked for the Shrovetide season. The piping revellers in this scene have Lebkuchen hearts hanging around their necks, their costumes are decorated with spiced honey biscuit shapes and Gingerbread Houses form unusual head-dresses.

Gingerbread Recipes Around the World

Canadian Gingerbread

A rich, traditional cake which can be iced with lemon glacé as an alternative.

YOU WILL NEED
275 g/10 oz plain flour
10 ml/2 tsp ground ginger
5 ml/1 tsp ground cinnamon
5 ml/1 tsp bicarbonate of soda
100 g/4 oz margarine or butter
100 g/4 oz light brown sugar
120 ml/4 fl oz black treacle
120 ml/4 fl oz golden syrup
150 ml/¼ pint hot water
2 eggs, beaten

— METHOD —

Sieve the flour, spices and bicarbonate of soda together in a bowl. Put the margarine or butter, sugar, treacle and golden syrup into a pan and stir until melted. Pour the melted syrups into the dry ingredients, together with the water and eggs. Mix well.

Pour the batter into a lined and greased 23-cm/9-in square shallow tin. Bake in a pre-heated oven at 180°C/350°F/Gas Mark 4 for 35–40 minutes. Keep for one day before cutting into squares to serve.

New England Maple Gingerbread

A firm favourite since the time of the early settlers, this gingerbread
is often served with a Maple Icing.

YOU WILL NEED
350 g/12 oz plain flour
5 ml/1 tsp bicarbonate of soda
10 ml/2 tsp ground ginger
pinch salt
1 egg
200 ml/7 fl oz maple syrup
200 ml/7 fl oz sour cream
100 g/4 oz butter, melted

ICING
225 g/8 oz icing sugar, sieved
25 g/1 oz softened butter
45 ml/3 tbsp maple syrup
15 ml/1 tbsp double cream

— METHOD —

Sieve the flour, bicarbonate of soda, ginger and salt together into a bowl. In another bowl beat together the egg, maple syrup and sour cream. Stir in the melted butter. Pour the syrup mixture into the dry ingredients and mix well together. Pour into a greased and base-lined 28-cm × 18-cm × 4-cm/11-in × 7-in × 1½-in tin.

Bake in a preheated oven at 180°C/350°F/Gas Mark 4 for about 30 minutes. Cool completely.

To make the icing, put all the ingredients into a bowl and beat until smooth. Spread icing over cake in swirls.

To serve, cut the gingerbread into bars.

Houston Gingerbread

*Very dark but light and fluffy in texture, this is
a sort of gingerbread "brownie".*

YOU WILL NEED

225 g/8 oz plain flour

2 tbsp cocoa powder

10 ml/2 tsp bicarbonate of soda

10 ml/2 tsp ground ginger

10 ml/2 tsp ground cinnamon

100 g/4 oz butter or margarine

175 g/6 oz castor sugar

2 eggs, separated

275 ml/10 fl oz molasses

200 ml/7 fl oz buttermilk

ICING

200 g/7 oz chocolate or chocolate-cake
covering

— METHOD —

Sieve the flour, cocoa powder, bicarbonate of soda and spices into a bowl. In another larger bowl, cream together the butter or margarine and sugar. Beat in the egg yolks and molasses. Alternately, fold the dry ingredients and buttermilk into the larger bowl. Whisk the egg whites until stiff and fold into the batter.

Spread the batter in a lined and greased 33-cm × 23-cm/13-in × 9-in shallow oblong baking tin. Bake in a preheated oven at 180°C/350°F/Gas Mark 4 for 25–30 minutes. Cool the cake slightly before turning out onto a cake rack to cool thoroughly.

Melt the chocolate gently in a bowl over a pan of hot water and spread over the cake. When set, cut the cake into squares to serve.

Mississippi Gingerbread

Sorghum molasses is usually used in this recipe. Sorghum is the sugary residue left when cane is cut down, milled, pressed and cooked each Autumn.

YOU WILL NEED
175 g/6 oz plain flour
5 ml/1 tsp bicarbonate of soda
5 ml/1 tsp ground ginger
5 ml/1 tsp ground allspice
5 ml/1 tsp ground cinnamon
100 g/4 oz butter or margarine
75 g/3 oz soft brown sugar
2 eggs, beaten
120 ml/4 fl oz molasses
100 ml/3½ fl oz buttermilk

TOPPING
50 g/2 oz soft brown sugar
25 g/1 oz plain flour
10 ml/2 tsp ground cinnamon
50 g/2 oz soft butter
100 g/4 oz mixed chopped nuts

— METHOD —

Sieve the flour, bicarbonate of soda and spices together into a bowl. In another bowl, cream together the butter or margarine and sugar. Beat in the eggs and molasses. Fold in the dry ingredients and buttermilk, stirring to combine well.

Spread the batter in a lined and greased 23-cm/9-in round sandwich tin. Bake in a preheated oven at 180°C/350°F/Gas Mark 4 for 20 minutes.

To make the topping, put all ingredients in a bowl and mix lightly with the fingers. After the gingerbread has been baking for 20 minutes, sprinkle the topping over the top and return to the oven for a further 10 minutes. Cool thoroughly before cutting in wedges to serve.

This gingerbread is delicious served as a dessert, with whipped cream or ice cream.

Louisiana Syrup Cake

*Sometimes called Gateau Sirop, this is a traditional favourite
in the deep South of America.*

YOU WILL NEED
350 g/12 oz plain flour
7.5 ml/1½ tsp baking powder
2.5 ml/½ tsp bicarbonate of soda
5 ml/1 tsp ground ginger
5 ml/1 tsp ground cinnamon
1.5 ml/¼ tsp grated nutmeg
1.5 ml/¼ tsp ground cloves
pinch salt
50 g/2 oz pecans, coarsely chopped
50 g/2 oz seedless raisins
120 ml/4 fl oz molasses
175 ml/6 fl oz golden syrup
200 ml/7 fl oz boiling water
50 ml/2 fl oz dark rum
100 g/4 oz butter or margarine
50 g/2 oz light soft brown sugar
2 eggs beaten

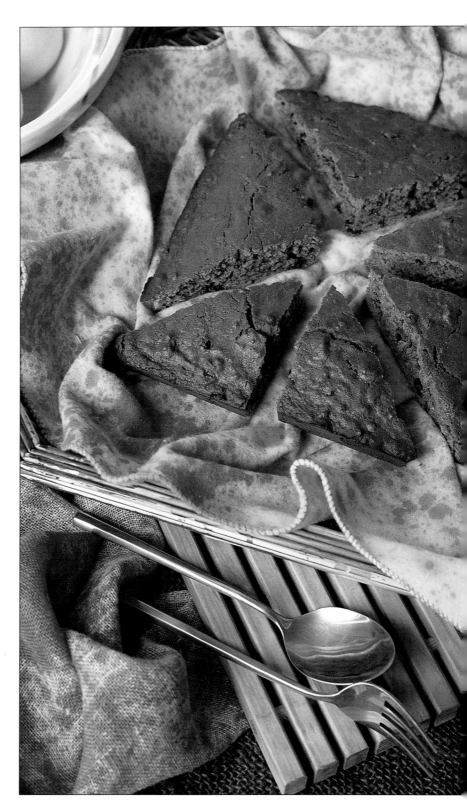

— METHOD —

Sieve the flour, baking powder, bicarbonate of soda, spices and salt together into a bowl. Add the pecans and raisins and mix gently into the flour mixture. Pour the molasses and syrup into a second bowl and stir in the boiling water, combining well. Stir in the rum.

In a large bowl, cream the butter or margarine and sugar together, then beat in the eggs. Beat in half the flour mixture, followed by half the syrup mixture. Add remaining flour mixture, then the rest of the syrup. Stir gently.

Pour the mixed batter carefully into a lined and greased 20-cm/8-in square cake tin. Bake the cake in a preheated oven at 180°C/350°F/Gas Mark 4 for about 1 hour. For best results, keep 1–2 days before cutting into large pieces. sections.

Muster Day Gingerbread

In New England before the Civil War, the first Tuesday of every June was Muster or Training Day. All men from 18 to 45 were required to go for military training and many of them took their families along. It became a festive occasion and gingerbread was an essential part of the day's menu.

YOU WILL NEED
50 g/2 oz soft brown sugar
75 g/3 oz molasses
5–10 ml/1–2 tsp ground ginger
2.5–5 ml/½–1 tsp ground cinnamon
1.5 ml/¼ tsp ground cloves
10 ml/2 tsp bicarbonate of soda
100 g/4 oz butter, cut into chunks
1 small egg
275–300 g/10–12 oz flour

— METHOD —

Put the sugar, molasses and spices into a pan and heat to boiling point. Stir in the bicarbonate of soda. Take off the heat and pour over the butter in a bowl. Stir until the butter has melted. Break the egg into the mixture and work in the flour. Mix lightly together, until it becomes a smooth dough.

Wrap the dough in polythene and refrigerate for a while. When chilled and stiffened slightly, roll out on non-stick paper and cut out with fancy biscuit cutters. Put on a greased baking sheet and bake in a preheated oven at 170°C/325°F/Gas Mark 3 for 8–10 minutes.

Amelia Simmons Gingerbread Loaf

Amelia Simmons, an early American cookery writer, made a rolled out gingerbread flavoured with the unusual ingredient of rose-water. She also gave a recipe for molasses gingerbread loaf which permanently changed the taste of American gingerbread. This recipe is best with butter, cream or ice cream.

YOU WILL NEED
275 g/10 oz plain flour
pinch salt
5 ml/1 tsp ground ginger
5 ml/1 tsp bicarbonate of soda
100 g/4 oz butter
100 g/4 oz brown sugar
2 eggs, separated
150 ml/5 fl oz sour cream
120 ml/4 fl oz molasses

— METHOD —

Sieve together the flour, salt, ginger and bicarbonate of soda. In another bowl, cream the butter and sugar together. Beat the egg yolks one by one into the creamed mixture. In a third bowl, beat together the sour cream and molasses. Fold the sour cream mixture into the butter mixture, alternating with the flour.

Beat the egg whites until stiff and fold into the cake mixture.

Pour the batter into a lined and greased 900-g/2-lb loaf tin and bake in a preheated oven at 170°C/325°F/Gas Mark 3 for about 50–60 minutes. Serve warm or at room temperature.

Jamaican Ginger Rub-Up Cake

Ginger has been grown in Jamaica since 1547 and today it is considered the world's finest. This ginger cake therefore uses freshly grated ginger root in place of ground ginger. In addition to a wonderful aroma, the ginger gives a mellow flavour to this deliciously moist cake.

YOU WILL NEED

225 g/8 oz plain flour

10 ml/2 tsp baking powder

2.5 ml/½ tsp bicarbonate of soda

5 ml/1 tsp allspice

2.5 ml/½ tsp ground nutmeg

225 g/8 oz butter

100 g/4 oz soft brown sugar

25 g/1 oz fresh ginger root, grated

120 ml/4 fl oz evaporated milk

120 ml/4 fl oz molasses

2 eggs, beaten

— METHOD —

Sieve the flour, baking powder, bicarbonate of soda and spices together in a bowl. Add the butter and sugar and rub lightly together with the fingers. Stir in the grated ginger root. Melt the evaporated milk and molasses together, but do not heat too much. Pour the molasses mixture into the flour, add the eggs, and stir gently together.

Pour the batter into a lined 900-g/2-lb loaf tin. Bake in a preheated oven at 180°C/350°F/Gas Mark 4 for about 50 minutes. Cool slightly in the tin before turning out onto a cake rack.

Cornish Fairings

In the week after Christmas in the market town of Launceston in Cornwall, a "maid-hiring" fair used to be held. Here one could buy Cornish Fairings made with honey and coloured with either saffron, liquorice or sandalwood. Decorated with almonds, marzipan, icing or gold leaf, these biscuits must have made a wonderful display in the vendors' trays.

YOU WILL NEED
225 g/8 oz plain flour
pinch salt
10 ml/2 tsp baking powder
10 ml/2 tsp bicarbonate of soda
10 ml/2 tsp ground mixed spice
15 ml/1 tbsp ground ginger
5 ml/1 tsp ground cinnamon
100 g/4 oz butter or margarine
100 g/4 oz castor sugar
60 ml/4 tbsp golden syrup, warmed

— METHOD —

Sieve the flour, salt, baking powder, bicarbonate of soda and spices into a bowl. Rub in the butter or margarine with the fingers. Stir in the sugar and the warmed syrup and mix to a stiff consistency.

Roll the dough into walnut-sized balls. Place well spaced on a greased baking sheet. Bake in a preheated oven at 200°C/400°F/Gas Mark 6 for about 10 minutes. Cool for a few minutes before transferring to a cooling rack.

Grantham Gingerbreads

These round puffy gingerbread biscuits should be "hollow and slightly dome-shaped, with a pleasing fawn tint".

YOU WILL NEED

250 g/9 oz self-raising flour
5 ml/1 tsp ground ginger
100 g/4 oz butter or hard margarine
350 g/12 oz castor sugar
1 egg, beaten

— METHOD —

In one bowl, sieve together the flour and the ginger. In another bowl, cream together the butter or margarine and sugar, then beat in the egg. Stir in the flour mixture and combine well. Roll the dough into walnut-sized balls.

Place the balls on a greased baking tray and bake in a preheated oven at 150°C/300°F/Gas Mark 2 for about 40 minutes until crisp, hollow and lightly browned.

Gingernuts

Originally from England, Gingernuts have become a firm favourite all over the world, especially enjoyable when dipped in a cup of tea.

YOU WILL NEED

100 g/4 oz self-raising flour
2.5 ml/½ tsp bicarbonate of soda
5–10 ml/1–2 tsp ground ginger
5 ml/1 tsp ground cinnamon
15 ml/1 tbsp castor sugar
50 g/2 oz butter or hard margarine
75 ml/3 fl oz golden syrup

— METHOD —

Sieve the flour, bicarbonate of soda and spices into a bowl. Stir in the sugar. Melt the butter or margarine and syrup together, pour onto the dry ingredients, and combine thoroughly. Roll the dough into balls. Place on a greased baking tray and flatten slightly with the palm of your hand. Bake in a preheated oven at 190°C/375°F/Gas Mark 5 for about 15 minutes. Cool and serve.

23

Welsh Gingerbread

Welsh gingerbread (Bara Sinsir) was traditionally sold at many old Welsh fairs.
Sometimes it did not even have ginger in it, but tasted as though it did!

YOU WILL NEED
450 g/1 lb plain flour
5 ml/1 tsp ground ginger
5 ml/1 tsp mixed spice
5 ml/1 tsp bicarbonate of soda
100 g/4 oz chopped mixed peel
450 g/1 lb clear honey
100 g/4 oz butter or margarine
50 g/2 oz soft brown sugar
2 eggs, beaten
50–150 ml/2–5 fl oz milk

GLAZE
60 ml/2 fl oz clear honey

— METHOD —

Sieve the flour, spices and bicarbonate of soda into a bowl. Stir in the mixed peel. In a saucepan, warm the honey, butter or margarine and sugar together until the sugar dissolves. Cool.

Make a well in the flour mixture and beat in the honey mixture, then the eggs and enough milk to make a thick batter. Pour the mixed batter carefully into a lined and greased 900 g/2 lb loaf tin.

Bake the gingerbread in a preheated oven at 170°C/325°F/Gas Mark 3 for about 1¼ hours. Remove the bread from the oven and brush with honey glaze while still hot. Keep for one day before cutting into slices. Welsh gingerbread may be spread with butter, honey or jam, if liked.

Grasmere Gingerbread

On a Saturday in early August, a rush-bearing ceremony is held in the Lake District. This dates back to a time when churches had stone or earth floors. Fresh hay or straw rushes were laid down to make kneeling easier, the church warmer, and to give a sweeter smell. Today many children take part in the service and are given pieces of specially-baked Grasmere gingerbread.

YOU WILL NEED

225 g/8 oz self-raising flour
75 g/3 oz sugar
5–10 ml/1–2 tsp ground ginger
100 g/4 oz butter or hard margarine
15 ml/1 tbsp golden syrup
2 egg yolks, beaten
100 g/4 oz mixed chopped peel

TOPPING
Egg white
30 ml/2 tbsp granulated sugar

— METHOD —

Put the flour, sugar and ginger into a bowl and mix together. In a pan, melt the butter or margarine and syrup. Take off the heat, cool slightly, and stir the egg yolks into the melted mixture. Gently beat the butter mixture into the flour.

Roll half the dough out to an oblong about 18 cm × 10 cm/7 in × 4 in on non-stick paper. Sprinkle the peel over the dough. Press the remaining dough over the top.

Lightly whisk the egg white and brush the top of the gingerbread with the froth and sprinkle with sugar. Bake the gingerbread in a preheated oven at 170°C/325°F/Gas Mark 3 for 20–30 minutes. When cool cut into small squares and serve.

Ginger-Rich Flapjacks

A modern favourite all over the world, especially good with a crunchy apple in children's lunch boxes.

YOU WILL NEED
50 g/2 oz butter or hard margarine
50 g/2 oz Demerara sugar
45 ml/3 tbsp golden syrup
100 g/4 oz rolled oats
2.5–5 ml/½–1 tsp ground ginger

— METHOD —
Put the butter or margarine, sugar and syrup into a pan and melt gently together. In a bowl mix together the oats and ginger. Pour the melted mixture onto the oats and stir well. Spoon the batter into a base-lined and greased 18-cm/7-in square shallow baking tin. Bake in a preheated oven at 180°C/350°F/Gas Mark 4 for 20–25 minutes. Leave to cool and slice.

Scottish Parliament Cakes

Traditionally cut into 10 cm/4 inch squares, these biscuits (Parlies) may be divided into smaller squares or indeed into any shape of your choice.

YOU WILL NEED
225 g/8 oz plain flour
10 ml/2 tsp ground ginger
100 g/4 oz butter
120 ml/4 fl oz black treacle
100 g/4 oz brown sugar

— METHOD —

Sieve the flour and ginger into a bowl. Put the butter, treacle and sugar into a heavy saucepan and melt gently. Cool slightly, then pour the warm mixture onto the flour. Mix together thoroughly until you have a dough, then roll out thinly into a large rectangle on non-stick paper.

Place the dough and paper on a baking tray and cut the dough, not quite through, into squares. Bake in a preheated oven at 170°C/325°F/Gas Mark 3 for 20 minutes.

Remove from the oven and break the biscuits apart while still warm. Leave until cold on a cooling rack.

Yorkshire Parkin

In Great Britain, this is often eaten on Guy Fawkes night – the 5th of November.
When making it in the North of England, it is popular to make an extra panful to serve
with apple sauce at tea-time.

YOU WILL NEED
225 g/8 oz plain flour
10 ml/2 level tsp baking powder
10 ml/2 level tsp ground ginger
50 g/2 oz butter or hard margarine
50 g/2 oz lard
225 g/8 oz medium oatmeal
100 g/4 oz castor sugar
175 ml/6 fl oz golden syrup
175 ml/6 fl oz black treacle
60 ml/4 tbsp milk

— METHOD —

In a bowl, sieve together the flour, baking powder and ginger. Rub in the fat and stir in the oatmeal and sugar.

In a saucepan, heat together the syrup and treacle until warm. Make a well in the dry ingredients and stir in the syrup mixture, together with the milk. Stir until smooth, then pour the batter into a greased and lined 20-cm/8-in square cake tin.

Bake in a preheated oven at 180°C/350°F/Gas Mark 4 for 45–60 minutes. Keep for a few days before serving.

Ormskirk Gingersnaps

This is a regional variation of the more commonly known "Brandy Snap".
These crispy tubes or cones were often sold at fairs in England
and are now popular at Christmas time.

YOU WILL NEED
150 g/5 oz plain flour
5 ml/1 tsp ground ginger
5 ml/1 tsp ground cinnamon
2.5 ml/½ tsp ground mace
Grated rind ½ lemon
175 g/6 oz butter
225 g/8 oz golden syrup
225 g/8 oz castor sugar

— METHOD —

Sieve the flour and spices into a bowl. Stir in the lemon rind. Melt the butter, syrup and sugar together in a pan. Pour the liquid into the flour mixture and blend until it is a soft dropping consistency.

Drop teaspoonfuls of the mixture onto a greased baking tray. Leave room between the biscuits to allow for spreading.

Bake the biscuits in a preheated oven at 180°C/350°F/Gas Mark 4 for about 7–10 minutes. Allow to cool for 1–2 minutes, then loosen with a palette knife. Roll the still soft "pancakes" around a greased wooden spoon handle. Leave until set, then twist the gingersnaps gently to remove.

If the biscuits cool too much while still on the sheet, return to the oven for a moment to soften them. Serve filled with whipped cream.

Edinburgh Gingerbread

Scotland has many variations of gingerbread, but this is one of the oldest and most popular.

YOU WILL NEED
450 g/1 lb plain flour
5–10 ml/1–2 tsp ground ginger
5–10 ml/1–2 tsp ground cinnamon
5–10 ml/1–2 tsp mixed spice
2.5 ml/½ tsp ground cloves
225 g/8 oz stoned dates, chopped
125 g/4 oz walnuts, chopped
225 g/8 oz butter or hard margarine
225 g/8 fl oz black treacle
175 g/6 oz brown sugar
4 eggs, beaten
5 ml/1 tsp bicarbonate of soda, dissolved in
15 ml/1 tbsp warm milk

— METHOD —

Sieve the flour and the spices together in a bowl. Add the dates and walnuts. Put the butter or margarine, treacle and sugar into a pan and heat gently until melted. Add the melted mixture, the eggs, and dissolved bicarbonate to the flour mixture and stir well to combine. Pour the mixture carefully into a lined 20-cm/8-in square cake tin.

Bake the cake in a preheated oven at 180°C/350°F/Gas Mark 4 for 20 minutes. Lower the heat to 160°C/325°F/Gas Mark 3 for a further 45–60 minutes. Keep for a couple of days before cutting in slices to serve.

Dutch Ginger Cake

This ginger cake typifies Dutch baking; lots of butter for a rich taste, glacé ginger and whole almonds for flavour.

YOU WILL NEED

225 g/8 oz plain flour
2.5 ml/½ tsp ground ginger
175 g/6 oz castor sugar
1 egg, beaten
175 g/6 oz unsalted butter, melted
75 g/3 oz chopped glacé ginger
a little milk
25 g/1 oz halved blanched almonds

— METHOD —

Sieve the flour and ground ginger together into a bowl. Stir in the sugar. Add the egg, butter and ginger and mix together well.

Spread the batter into a greased and lined 20-cm/8-in round sandwich tin. Brush the top with milk and decorate with almonds. Bake in a preheated oven at 180°C/350°F/Gas Mark 4 for 35–40 minutes. Remove from the oven and when cool cut in wedges to serve.

Dutch Spice Biscuits

These biscuits are traditionally eaten on the feast of St Nicholas, 6th December. The name comes from the Latin word for mirror, because the wooden moulds in which the biscuit is usually made is the mirror image of the biscuit. The traditional design shows a man and a woman, representing a King and Queen or a lover and his lass.

YOU WILL NEED
175 g/6 oz butter
200 g/7 oz soft brown sugar
50 g/2 oz finely chopped nuts (almonds or mixed nuts)
275 g/10 oz flour
5 ml/1 tsp ground cinnamon
2.5 ml/½ tsp ground ginger
1.25 ml/¼ tsp ground nutmeg
1.25 ml/¼ tsp ground cloves
pinch ground mace
2.5 ml/½ tsp ground aniseed, or 2 drops anise oil (optional)
1.25 ml/¼ tsp baking powder
30 ml/2 tbsp milk

DECORATION
whole blanched almonds
currants

— **METHOD** —

In a bowl, cream the butter and sugar together until light and fluffy. Stir in the nuts. In another bowl, sieve the flour, spices and baking powder together. Add the flour mixture little by little to the butter mixture, alternating with the milk and stirring continuously. When the batter becomes stiffer, gently knead in any remaining flour by hand. The resultant dough should be firm, otherwise it will spread too much in baking. Add more flour if the dough is too slack.

Divide the dough into four. Take one piece and shape as follows: remove a quarter of the dough and shape into a round head and simple crown about 6-mm/¼-in thick. Place on non-stick paper on a baking tray. From the remaining dough, pinch off a piece just smaller

than half, and pat out an oval body shape. Put on the tray and attach to the head. Shape the remaining piece into a large skirt or two legs and attach to body. With a teaspoon, fork and knife, make patterns on the King or Queen. Place whole and slivered almonds on the body and crown. Add currants for eyes. Make similar figures with the remaining three pieces of dough. The patterns should not be too intricate as the dough rises slightly in cooking and a bold pattern is better.

Chill for 30 minutes, then bake in a preheated oven at 190°C/375°F/Gas Mark 5 for about 15 minutes. Allow to become cold before removing from the non-stick paper.

Scandinavian Spice Biscuits

This recipe is made in Scandinavia especially at Christmas-time. Fancy Christmas shapes are cut out and simply decorated with white icing and then hung on the tree.

YOU WILL NEED
125 g/4 oz butter
90 g/3½ oz Demerara sugar
200 ml/7 fl oz golden syrup or molasses
5 ml/1 level tsp ground ginger
5 ml/1 level tsp ground cinnamon
2.5 ml/½ level tsp ground cloves
10 ml/2 tsp bicarbonate of soda
1 egg
500 g/1 lb 2 oz plain flour, sieved

TO DECORATE
Royal icing

— **METHOD** —

Cut the butter into pieces. Put the sugar, syrup or molasses and spices into a saucepan and bring to the boil. Take off the heat, add the bicarbonate of soda, pour the mixture over the butter, stirring until the butter has melted.

Beat the egg into the butter mixture, then slowly blend in the sieved flour.

Combine thoroughly, then use the hands to knead the mixture lightly, to form a smooth manageable dough. Roll out about one quarter of the dough at a time between sheets of non-stick or waxed paper, keeping the rest in a polythene bag. Cut out fancy shapes or angels (as described below). Bake in a preheated oven at 170°C/325°F/Gas Mark 3 for 10–15 minutes. Allow to cool.

To make Christmas angels, roll out two-thirds of the dough and cut into rectangles, approximately 5 × 8 cm/2 × 3 in. From the top corners of each rectangle, cut 2 triangles and rearrange to form wings (see picture below). Roll the remaining dough into small balls for the heads. Press onto the top of the body and flatten slightly with your hand. Bake as for the main recipe.

When cold, outline the angel shape with royal icing, using a No. 2 plain writing nozzle.

French Gingerbread

This is the French equivalent of gingerbread, otherwise known as Pain d'Epice. *In some regional variations the recipes include chopped glacé fruits and nuts.*

YOU WILL NEED
225 g/8 oz plain flour
225 g/8 oz rye flour
2.5 ml/½ tsp salt
10 ml/2 tsp ground ginger
5 ml/1 tsp ground allspice
25 g/1 oz fresh yeast
300 ml/½ pint lukewarm water
5 ml/1 tsp sugar
225 ml/8 fl oz honey
50 g/2 oz chopped glacé fruits, optional

— METHOD —

Put the flours, salt and spices into a bowl and mix together. In another bowl, dissolve the yeast in the water and sugar. Pour the yeast mixture into the flour mixture and stir with a spoon. Work to a firm dough, adding extra flour if needed. Knead on a floured surface until the dough is smooth and no longer sticky. Put in a bowl, cover and leave in a warm place until double in size.

Punch the dough down and knead in the honey and fruits. Put into a lined and greased loaf tin, leave in a warm place until risen. Bake in a preheated oven at 225°C/425°F/ Gas Mark 7 for about 30 minutes.

Lebkuchen

This is similar to the original Nuremberg gingerbread and is equally mouthwatering warm or cold.

YOU WILL NEED

275 g/10 oz flour
2.5 ml/½ tsp baking powder
2.5 ml/½ tsp ground ginger
2.5 ml/½ tsp ground cinnamon
2.5 ml/½ tsp ground cloves
1.25 ml/¼ tsp ground nutmeg
175 g/6 oz shelled almonds, ground
50 g/2 oz finely chopped candied orange
and lemon peel
2 eggs
125 g/4 oz castor sugar
350 ml/12 fl oz honey
90 ml/6 tbsp milk

ICING

175 g/6 oz icing sugar
2.5 ml/½ tsp almond essence
5 ml/1 tsp lemon juice
water

— METHOD —

Line a Swiss roll tin with greaseproof paper, brush lightly with oil and put aside. In a bowl, sieve the flour, baking powder and spices together. Stir in the almonds and chopped peel. Break the eggs into another bowl, add the sugar, and whisk until the mixture is light and thick, leaving a trail when the whisk is lifted. Whisk in the honey and milk followed by the flour mixture.

Pour the batter into the prepared tin. Bake in a preheated oven at 200°C/400°F/Gas Mark 6 for 15–20 minutes.

To make the icing, put the icing sugar into a bowl. Add the essence, lemon juice and enough water to mix to a thick consistency. Brush the icing over the hot Lebkuchen. Cut into bars to serve.

Light German Gingernuts

In old German recipes baking powder was actually powdered hartshorn, made from the antlers of harts and deer. The modern equivalent is ammonium carbonate which is still used in parts of Germany and Europe for the very crisp texture it imparts.

YOU WILL NEED
3 eggs
175 g/6 oz castor sugar
450 g/1 lb flour
1.25 ml/¼ tsp baking powder
pinch salt
pinch white pepper
5 ml/1 tsp ground cinnamon
large pinch ground ginger
large pinch ground cloves
25 g/1 oz ground almonds
50 g/2 oz finely chopped mixed peel,
optional

— METHOD —

Put the eggs and sugar into a bowl and whisk until very thick and frothy. In another bowl sieve the flour, baking powder, salt, pepper and spices together. Blend the flour and spices into the whisked mixture. Sprinkle in the almonds and peel; knead lightly to form a soft dough.

Roll out the dough to 5-mm/¼-in thick on a floured board. Cut out small fancy shapes. Place the biscuits on non-stick paper on a baking tray. Bake the gingernuts (pfeffernüsse) in a preheated oven at 180°C/350°F/Gas Mark 4 for about 10–15 minutes. Cool on a wire rack. These biscuits are very hard and crisp and should be stored with a piece of apple or orange to soften them.

Dark German Gingernuts

A dark, spicy gingerbread or Pfeffernüsse used to make biscuits or cut into larger pieces for building Gingerbread Houses. The difference between this recipe and the previous one is the absence of baking powder.

YOU WILL NEED

100 g/4 oz butter or margarine or white vegetable fat
100 g/4 oz soft brown sugar
1 egg
100 g/4 oz black treacle
2–3 drops anise oil in 5 ml/1 tsp water, optional
400 g/14 oz flour
2.5 ml/½ tsp bicarbonate of soda
pinch salt
2.5 ml/½ tsp ground ginger
2.5 ml/½ tsp ground cloves

— METHOD —

In a bowl, cream together the butter and sugar. Beat in the egg, treacle and anise oil. In another bowl, sieve together the flour, bicarbonate of soda, salt and spices. Stir the flour into the creamed mixture, gradually blending in by hand. Mix to a smooth dough. Either use for moulding, or roll out and cut out small fancy shapes with cutters.

Place the moulded or cut biscuits on a greased baking sheet and bake in a preheated oven at 180°C/350°F/Gas Mark 4 for 10–12 minutes. Cool on a wire rack.

The biscuits will harden on cooling. It is traditional to store these biscuits in an airtight tin, with a slice of apple to "mellow" them.

Russian Spice Biscuits

This traditional Russian biscuit or Pryaniki *was often made in the shape of a pig,
cockerel or other farm animal and was sold at village fairs.*

YOU WILL NEED
225 g/8 oz plain flour
1.5 ml/¼ tsp ground ginger
1.5 ml/¼ tsp ground cloves
1.5 ml/¼ tsp ground nutmeg
1.5 ml/¼ tsp ground cinnamon
pinch ground cardamom
1.5 ml/¼ tsp baking powder
2 eggs
100 g/4 oz soft brown sugar
15 ml/1 tbsp milk

———

GLAZE
75 ml/3 fl oz water
175 g/6 oz castor sugar
1 large egg white

— METHOD —

Sieve the flour, spices and baking powder into a bowl. In another bowl, beat the eggs and sugar together with an electric beater or hand whisk, until the mixture is thick and fluffy. Mix in the flour and spices. Gather the mixture together to form a dough, adding the milk if necessary.

Roll the dough out on a lightly-floured board and cut out desired shapes. Place the "animals" on a greased baking sheet and bake in a preheated oven at 180°C/350°F/Gas Mark 4 for about 10 minutes. Cool on a wire rack.

To make the glaze, put the water and sugar into a pan. Heat slowly, stirring until the sugar has dissolved. Bring to the boil. Boil for a few minutes to form a syrup – the mixture should *not* begin to go brown. Whisk the egg white in a bowl until stiff. Pour the syrup onto the egg white, beating continuously. Working quickly, coat the biscuits with the icing, before it becomes too solid. Leave to dry and serve.

Lithuanian Mushroom Biscuits

These unusual little cakes or Grybai come from Lithuania. They are shaped and iced to look like mushrooms and are very popular with children.

YOU WILL NEED

25 g/1 oz unsalted butter
50 g/2 oz soft brown sugar
1 egg
120 ml/4 fl oz honey
25 g/1 oz sour cream
350 g/12 oz flour
5 ml/1 tsp bicarbonate of soda
5 ml/1 tsp ground cinnamon
2.5 ml/½ tsp ground ginger
2.5 ml/½ tsp ground cloves
2.5 ml/½ tsp ground nutmeg
1.5 ml/¼ tsp ground cardamon
5 ml/1 tsp finely-grated lemon rind
5 ml/1 tsp finely-grated orange rind

ICING

225 g/8 oz icing sugar, sieved
30 ml/2 tbsp strained lemon juice
30 ml/2 tbsp water
10 ml/2 tsp cocoa powder

— METHOD —

In a bowl, cream the butter and sugar together. Beat in the egg, then the honey and sour cream. In another bowl, sieve together the flour, bicarbonate of soda and spices. Add to the creamed mixture a little at a time, stirring continuously. Add the grated rinds and stir to a smooth dough. Wrap the dough in waxed paper and chill until firm.

Cut off about two-thirds of the dough. Shape into balls and push the thumb in the centre to make an indent like a mushroom. Put – rounded-side up – onto a greased baking tray. Shape the remaining dough into stems, and place on the tray.

Bake the biscuits in a preheated oven at 180°C/350°F/Gas Mark 4 for about 10 minutes. Cool.

To make the icing, put the icing sugar in a bowl. Stir in the lemon juice and enough water to give a coating consistency. Divide the icing into two bowls. Leave the icing in one bowl and add the cocoa power to the other. Coat the mushroom caps with the brown icing. Coat the mushroom stems with white icing. Allow to set, then attach the stems to the caps with the remaining icing.

Polish Honey Cake

More of a honey spice cake, Piernik *recipes do not always contain ginger,*
but a mixture of spices.

YOU WILL NEED
450 g/1 lb plain flour
10 ml/2 tsp baking powder
2.5 ml/½ tsp ground ginger
2.5 ml/½ tsp ground cinnamon
2.5 ml/½ tsp ground cloves
2.5 ml/½ tsp ground allspice
grated rind ½ orange
50 g/2 oz chopped hazelnuts or walnuts
50 g/2 oz raisins
50 g/2 oz chopped dried figs
50 g/2 oz chopped angelica
450 g/1 lb honey
175 g/6 oz castor sugar
75 g/3 oz butter
4 egg yolks
10 ml/2 tsp instant coffee, dissolved in a
little water, *or* 10 ml/2 tsp caramel
4 egg whites

— METHOD —

Sieve the flour, baking powder and spices into a bowl. Stir in the orange rind, nuts, raisins, figs and angelica. Put the honey, sugar and butter into a pan and heat until completely melted. Cool slightly.

Add the melted mixture, egg yolks and coffee or caramel to the flour and mix well. In a bowl, whisk the egg whites until very stiff and then fold into the mixture.

Pour the batter into a lined 23-cm/9-in round cake tin (or very large loaf tin). Bake in a preheated oven at 180°C/350°F/Gas Mark 4 for 1–1¼ hours.

If liked, you can slice the Piernik and sandwich the halves together with thick jam. You can also ice the top with chocolate or thick chocolate icing.

Moravian Ginger Biscuits

The Moravians were quick to use the ginger and other spices brought to Philadelphia in the 18th century. The biscuits below would be cut out in animal shapes, or cut into squares.

YOU WILL NEED

75 g/3 oz butter or margarine

50 g/2 oz brown sugar

30 ml/2 tbsp molasses

175 g/6 oz flour

5 ml/1 tsp grated lemon rind

5 ml/1 tsp ground ginger

2.5 ml/½ tsp bicarbonate of soda

2.5 ml/½ tsp ground cinnamon

1.5 ml/¼ tsp ground cloves

1.5 ml/¼ tsp ground allspice

pinch ground nutmeg

———

DECORATION

Demerara sugar

— METHOD —

Put the butter or margarine, sugar and molasses into a pan and warm until melted. Remove from the heat, stir in the remaining ingredients and mix together until stiff. Wrap the dough in polythene and chill until firm.

Roll the chilled dough out on a lightly-floured board. Cut out into squares, animal shapes or as you wish. Put the biscuits on a greased baking tray and sprinkle the tops with Demerara sugar. Bake in a preheated oven at 190°C/375°F/Gas Mark 5 for about 8 minutes. Remove to a cake rack to cool thoroughly.

South African Almond Ginger Biscuits

The origins of this recipe otherwise known as Soetkoekies, are unclear but it probably travelled to South Africa with the early Dutch settlers.

YOU WILL NEED

350 g/12 oz plain flour
5 ml/1 tsp baking powder
5 ml/1 tsp ground ginger
5 ml/1 tsp ground cinnamon
1.5 ml/¼ tsp ground cloves
pinch salt
75 g/3 oz butter
175 g/6 oz dark soft brown sugar
1 egg, beaten
60 ml/2 fl oz port, sherry or Madeira
50 g/2 oz ground almonds

TO DECORATE
blanched halved almonds
1 egg white, beaten with
15 ml/1 tbsp water

— METHOD —

Sieve the flour, baking powder, spices and salt together into a bowl. In another bowl, cream together the butter and sugar and beat in the egg. Stir in the wine and ground almonds, and little by little beat in the dry mixture. Mix to a soft but not sticky dough, adding more flour if necessary.

Roll the dough out to 0.5-cm/¼-in thick on a floured surface or on non-stick paper. Using a 5-cm/2-in flower or round cutter, stamp out the biscuits. Place the biscuits on a greased baking tray with space between them and put a halved almond in the centre of each. Brush each biscuit with a little egg white.

Bake in a preheated oven at 180°C/350°F/ Gas Mark 4 for 10–15 minutes, or until golden brown. Serve.

42

Decorating and Building with Gingerbread

Construction Gingerbread

The following gingerbread and icing recipes are those you are most likely to need when making gingerbread houses, people and other amusing – and edible – delights.

YOU WILL NEED
725 g/1½ lb plain flour
2.5 ml/½ tsp bicarbonate of soda
2.5 ml/½ tsp salt
10 ml/2 tsp ground ginger
10 ml/2 tsp ground cinnamon
5 ml/1 tsp ground nutmeg
5 ml/1 tsp ground cloves
225 g/8 oz solid white vegetable
shortening
225 g/8 oz castor sugar
300 g/10 oz black treacle or
molasses
2 eggs, beaten

— METHOD —

In a bowl, sieve together the flour, bicarbonate of soda, salt and spices. Put the shortening in a pan and melt slowly. Add the sugar and treacle or molasses and mix until runny. Pour the fat mixture into the flour, and add the eggs. Mix well together until stiff, then knead lightly with the hands until smooth.

Wrap the dough tightly in a plastic bag. Use as desired.

If the gingerbread is used for large pieces such as walls, roofs, etc, the cooking time will be 10–14 minutes. Smaller pieces will need less time. Bake in a preheated oven at 180°C/350°F/Gas Mark 4.

Golden Gingerbread

If a darker-coloured gingerbread is desired, then replace half or all of the golden syrup with black treacle. Be sure to measure the syrup or treacle accurately with measuring spoons or the dough might spread when it is baked.

YOU WILL NEED

350 g/12 oz plain flour

10 ml/2 tsp ground ginger

5 ml/1 tsp ground cinnamon

2.5 ml/½ tsp bicarbonate of soda

100 g/4 oz butter

175 g/6 oz soft brown sugar

60 ml/4 tbsp golden syrup

1 egg, beaten

— METHOD —

1 Sieve the flour, spices and bicarbonate of soda into a bowl. Rub in the butter with the fingers until the mixture resembles fine breadcrumbs.

2 Stir in the sugar. In a saucepan, warm the syrup to make it runny.

3 Add the syrup and the beaten egg to the flour mixture; mix to a soft dough. If it is too sticky, add a little more flour.

4 Knead the dough lightly until smooth.

5 Roll out as desired. If the dough is rolled out thinly, a crisp texture will be obtained. If rolled out thickly, a softer texture will result. Bake in a preheated oven at 190°C/375°F/Gas Mark 5. Most items will take 8–10 minutes to cook. Smaller items will need less time and large pieces will take slightly longer.

1

2

3

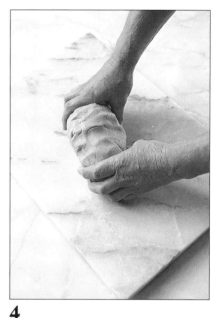

4

5

HANDY HINTS FOR CUTTING AND BAKING

☐ For small items, such as biscuits, it is sufficient to roll the dough out on a lightly-floured surface. They can then be lifted carefully with a palette knife onto a non-stick paper-lined tray.

☐ For large items it is best to roll the dough out on non-stick paper. Lift this onto a baking sheet and then cut out the design. This way, very little distortion takes place, which is important in the case of constructions.

☐ It is also advisable to roll the dough out between two lengths of dowel. A dowel thickness of 6 mm/¼ in is suitable for large items and 3 mm/⅛ in for small items. The dowels are placed on either side of the dough and the rolling pin rests on them, so that a perfectly even thickness and surface for the dough is achieved.

☐ When rolling out, try not to sprinkle any extra flour on the dough, as this can create white areas·which show up after the dough has been cooked.

☐ To use the cardboard patterns, place the pattern on top of the dough and cut carefully around, using a sharp knife. Endeavour not to "drag" the knife when cutting. Before using again, dust the template with flour and brush off. Angle the patterns around earlier cut-outs, when possible, to make best use of the dough. Gently remove the excess dough, knead into a ball and wrap in polythene. In some projects the excess dough needs to be rolled out again to be sure to obtain all the pieces.

☐ After baking, while the pieces are still warm, lay the cardboard templates on top and trim away any parts that have expanded too much. This is really only necessary for houses and other constructions where a perfect fit is required.

☐ If holes or slits have slightly closed during baking, then re-open them while the gingerbread is still warm.

☐ Cool the gingerbread on a wire rack. Do not remove from the non-stick paper until quite cold.

ABOVE Illustrated here is a small selection of the numerous biscuit and gingerbread cutters available. If you do not have time to make a template, a cutter will work just as well.

MAKING TEMPLATES

1 Put a piece of tracing paper over the pattern you wish to copy, and attach with tape or paper clips.

2 Carefully copy the outline in pencil.

3 Using a piece of carbon paper, transfer the design onto light-weight cardboard. Again use tape or paperclips to secure the tracing paper and carbon, so they do not move. The reverse side of old cereal cartons is ideal.

4 Cut out the cardboard template using sharp scissors, or a craft knife.

5 When cutting out large pieces for gingerbread houses, draughts-man's square paper is very useful, either on its own if stiff enough, or pasted over the light-weight cardboard. If this is not available, then use a ruler and something right-angled, such as a book, to ensure that all the walls have exact right angles. This is very important if the baked gingerbread pieces are to fit exactly together.

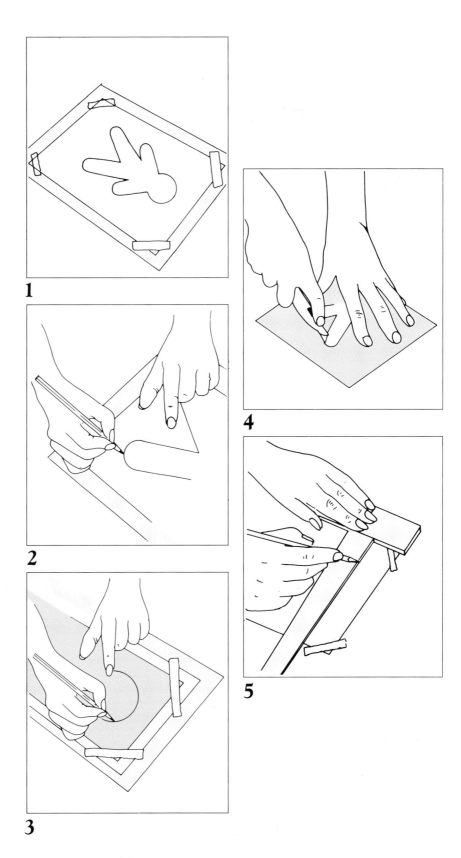

1

2

3

4

5

Making Icing

ROYAL ICING

This can be prepared to different consistencies, depending on the finish that is required. Make the icing in small amounts and keep in a bowl covered by a damp cloth or cling film, as it dries out very quickly.

YOU WILL NEED
1 egg white
175–225 g/6–8 oz icing sugar, sieved

— METHOD —

Beat the egg white. Gradually beat in the icing sugar, a little at a time, beating out any lumps.

For piping, the icing should be of a soft-peak consistency. For coating or flowing icing, add enough water so that the icing becomes the consistency of double cream.

For glazing, the icing should be even thinner, more the consistency of single cream.

ROYAL ICING "CEMENT"

This is very similar to Royal Icing, but is thicker in consistency and is used to stick edges together and candies onto Gingerbread Houses.

YOU WILL NEED
45 ml/3 tbsp meringue powder
100 ml/3½ fl oz warm water
450 g/1 lb icing sugar, sieved
2.5 ml/½ tsp cream of tartar

— METHOD —

Beat well together the meringue powder and the warm water. Stir in the icing sugar and cream of tartar. Beat vigorously with an electric beater for 3–4 minutes. When it is ready, keep it in a tightly-covered container until ready for use.

GLACÉ ICING

YOU WILL NEED
225 g/8 oz icing sugar, sieved
Boiling water

— METHOD —

Add to the icing sugar enough boiling water to make a fairly stiff coating consistency. The icing should hold a trail when dropped from a spoon, and should slowly sink to its own level.

Gingerbread Men and Women

MINI-PEOPLE GIFT BOX COOKIES

YOU WILL NEED
Golden Gingerbread dough
(see page 45)
Royal Icing, coating consistency
(see page 48)
Royal Icing, piping consistency
(see page 48)
Red food colouring
Gift boxes
Tiny gingerbread people cutters

— METHOD —

1 Roll out the dough and cut out the mini-people with cutter or template. Carefully remove the excess dough.

2 Bake for about 8 minutes. Cool completely.

3 Divide the coating Royal Icing in half. Colour one half of the coating icing with red food-colouring. Place the cookies on a wire rack.

4 Coat half the cookies with the red icing and the other half with the plain white icing. Allow to dry.

5 Divide the Royal Icing for piping in half. Colour one half of the piping icing with red food colouring. Using a small plain writing nozzle, pipe features and outline clothes in red icing on all the white-iced figures. Using white Royal Icing, pipe features and outline clothes on all the red-iced people. Allow to dry.

6 Pack in rows in suitable sweet boxes.

1

2

3

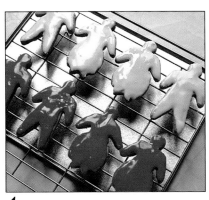

4

5

6

MR AND MRS SANTA COOKIES

YOU WILL NEED
Golden Gingerbread dough
(see page 45)
Royal Icing, coating consistency
(see page 48)
Royal Icing, piping consistency
(see page 48)
Red food colouring

— METHOD —

1 Using a medium or large gingerbread man cutter or template (see page 92), cut out and bake the dough people. Allow to cool.

2 Colour the coating Royal Icing with red food colouring. Put a little red icing into a piping bag. Outline red clothes on the figures.

3 Use the remaining red icing to "flood" the areas inside the piping. Allow to dry.

4 Decorate by using a small rosette pipe for a fluffy effect and the white Royal Icing of piping consistency, pipe the hair, beard and fur trims etc on Mr and Mrs Santa. Using a small plain writing nozzle, and white and red icing, pipe features onto the faces.

1

3

2

4

COUNTRY GIRLS AND BOYS

YOU WILL NEED
Golden Gingerbread dough
(see page 45)
Purchased fondant icing
Currants
Royal Icing, piping consistency
(see page 48)
Royal Icing, coating consistency
(see page 48)
Blue food colouring
Yellow food-colouring

— METHOD —

1 Roll out the dough and, using a gingerbread man cutter or template, cut out the figures.

2 Before baking, press the currants in for the hair and eyes, and pieces of glacé cherry for the mouth. Bake. Allow to cool.

3 Using a little white Royal Icing of piping consistency, pipe outlines of the clothes onto the gingerbread figures. Divide the Royal Icing of coating consistency between two small bowls. Mix in the food colouring. Use these icings to "flood" the areas inside the piping. Allow to dry.

4 To make the waistcoats and aprons, roll out the purchased fondant icing. Cut out 2 small rectangles for each Country boy. Scallop the bottom of the waistcoat with the aid of a fluted cutter. Make decorative holes with a skewer. Attach the waistcoats to the gingerbread boys with a little Royal

Icing. Cut the apron pieces as shown. Again trim the top and bottom with a fluted cutter and make holes with a skewer. Attach the aprons to the gingerbread girls with Royal Icing. If liked, small white polka dots may be piped onto the girls "dresses", using white Royal Icing and a plain nozzle.

1

2

3

4

Children's Corner

SMILEY FACES

YOU WILL NEED
Golden Gingerbread dough
(see page 45)
Royal Icing, coating consistency
(see page 48)
Various food colourings
Various sweets such as:
"Smarties"
marshmallows
mints
chocolate dots
jelly beans
shoelace liquorice
liquorice all-sorts
dolly mixtures etc.

1

2

— METHOD —

1 Roll out the Golden Gingerbread. Cut out large 9–10-cm/3½–4-in circles using a glass or tea-cup. Bake the circles according to Golden Gingerbread instructions. Allow to cool.

2 Make 2 or 3 different coloured Royal Icings and use to ice the biscuits.

3 Use sweets to make "smily faces" as illustrated, or create your own.

3

LARGE LETTERS AND NUMBERS

1

1
— METHOD FOR —
— SAUSAGE LETTERS —

Roll out long sausages 7 mm/¼ in thick for small letters, 1 cm/½ in thick for large letters. Shape into letters on non-stick paper. Make initials, names, messages and so on. Bake as instructed under Golden Gingerbread. When cool, the letters may be coated with melted chocolate or cake covering.

2

2
— METHOD FOR CUT-OUT LETTERS —

Draw out large capital letters on a piece of card. For example "G" for Grandpa or any number, perhaps for a birthday. Cut out and use as a template. Using the templates, cut out the letters. Bake as instructed under Golden Gingerbread. Cool. When cold, ice the letters with Royal or Glacé Icing. Decorate as desired with sweets, sugar flowers etc.

3

3
— METHOD FOR KNOBBLY LETTERS —

Roll out lots of small balls about 1 cm/½ in in diameter. On non-stick paper, shape the letters by placing balls edge-to-edge as illustrated. Bake as instructed under Golden Gingerbread.

PIGS

YOU WILL NEED
Golden Gingerbread dough
(see page 45)

— METHOD —

1 To make a pig, roll out the dough onto non-stick paper. Cut out a circle about 4 cm/1½ in in diameter, and an oval of approximately 9 cm/3½ in in length. Cut out two 2.5-cm/1-in squares. Cut each square almost to the top and pull slightly apart. These are the legs.

1

54

2

4

3

5

6

2 Put the legs on a piece of non-stick paper. Place the oval body on top and press lightly to join. If the dough is dry, use a little water to attach the pieces.

3 Put the circle on the body as shown, to represent the head.

4 Cut out a small circle about 2 cm/ ¾ in and cut in half. These are the ears. Stick onto head and fold each ear over.

5 Take a small piece of dough and roll into a tapering sausage. Curl it to form a tail and attach it to the body. Roll a thick sausage about 1 cm/½ in in diameter, and cut into pieces. Put one piece on the head to form the nose and the rest on the body as spots. Using a skewer, mark the eyes, nostrils and mouth.

6 Bake as instructed under Golden Gingerbread. Try making one very large "Mummy" pig, and lots of small baby piglets.

SHEEP

YOU WILL NEED
Golden Gingerbread dough
(see page 45)

— METHOD —

1 To make a sheep, roll out the dough onto non-stick paper. Carefully cut out a 4.5-cm/1¾-in circle for the head, and a 7.5-cm/3-in circle for the body.

2 Put the body on a piece of non-stick paper and push the sides gently with your fingers to make the circle "wavy". Attach the head to the body with a little water. Roll out two small

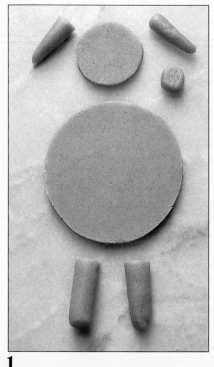

1

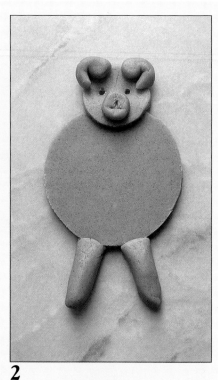

2

3

sausages for legs and attach to the body. Roll out two tapering sausages and curl round to make horns. Attach to the head. Roll a little ball for the nose and mouth. Flatten it slightly and attach it to the face.

3 Put some gingerbread dough into a garlic press and push through onto the body of the sheep to make the woolly coat. Put a few curls on the head as well. Use a skewer to mark the eyes, nose and mouth.

4 Finally, bake the sheep as instructed under Golden Gingerbread.

4

HANDFUL OF LOVE

This delightful idea is the perfect way to say "Happy Mother's Day" or "Happy Birthday – I love you" or even "Happy St Valentine's Day" to a sweetheart.

YOU WILL NEED
Golden Gingerbread dough
(see page 45)
Blanched almonds, optional
Red Glacé Icing (see page 48)
Royal Icing, piping consistency
(see page 48)
Sweets, silver balls etc (optional)

— **METHOD** —

1 Put your hand on a piece of thin card and draw round it. Cut out and use as a template. Roll out the gingerbread on non-stick paper. Cut out the hand from the gingerbread, using the pattern. At the same time, cut out a small heart using a cutter or a hand-cut heart template. Place the heart between the first finger and thumb. If liked, press almonds in the fingers to represent nails. Bake as instructed under Golden Gingerbread.

2 When cold, ice the heart with red Glacé Icing. Allow to set. Using Royal Icing in a piping bag fitted with a small plain nozzle, pipe a message on the heart. If liked, stick sweets on with Royal Icing to represent a bracelet and rings.

1

2

57

MINI-HOUSES

These little houses are very easy to make. You could present them as gifts on silver boards wrapped in clear cellophane, or you can make several different designs with exciting decorations and design a whole street to display on a Christmas or Birthday table.

> **YOU WILL NEED**
> Golden Gingerbread dough
> (see page 45)
> Royal Icing "Cement"
> (see page 48)
> A selection of small sweets
> Nuts (optional)

— METHOD —

Trace the pattern and transfer onto thin card. Roll out the gingerbread on non-stick paper and, using the templates, cut out the pieces. Cut out the doors and windows. Windows can be square, arched, oblong, diamond, heart-shaped, and doors can be square, arched or even round! Keep the piece cut out for the door and bake it separately. If nuts are to be used in your design, then press them into the dough.

1 Bake as instructed under Golden Gingerbread. (Any leftover dough can be made into small trees, people etc.) After baking, trim the edges of the gingerbread if necessary.

2 To assemble the house, spread a little thick Royal Icing "cement" on the narrow ends of the side pieces and join to the front and the back pieces. Allow to dry for a couple of hours.

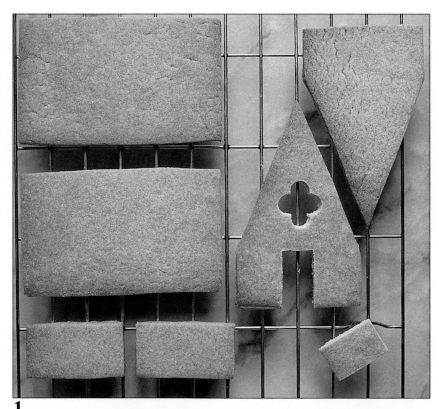

1

2

3

3 Spread Royal Icing on one narrow edge of each of the roof pieces. Spread Royal Icing on the top edge of the front and back. Attach the roof pieces, making sure there is plenty of icing at the top where they join.

4 Using Royal Icing, attach the door in an open position.

5 The house can now be decorated. Using Royal Icing, stick on the small sweets. For the roof "tiles", there is a choice of thin chocolate mints, chocolate flake or small flat biscuits etc which can be stuck on with Royal Icing. Allow to dry. Thin the Royal Icing with a little lemon juice, and drizzle circles onto the window ledges and roof edges. Spread some icing on a

small silver board and place the house on top in position. If you have made trees or figures, then attach them to the board with Royal Icing.

4

5

Fans

BASIC FAN

YOU WILL NEED
Golden Gingerbread dough
(see page 45)
Royal Icing
(see page 48)
Food colourings
Small sugar flowers

— METHOD —

1 Make a template for your fan (see page 93 for Sweetheart fan). Otherwise use a plate or a compass and draw almost a semi-circle. Make a fancy edge to the fan either free hand or by using a scalloped plate or a pie-cutter. Draw the two sides with a ruler. Then make another small semi-circle for the handle, using a small glass, egg cup or something similar.

2 Roll out the gingerbread on non-stick paper and use the template to cut out the fans. Cut out small shapes from the fan dough such as hearts, diamonds etc. Small circles can be cut out with an apple corer, the end of an icing nozzle, or pieces of macaroni. Small holes can also be made with a skewer. Bake as instructed under Golden Gingerbread.

3 Decorate with piped coloured Royal Icing, sugar flowers etc depending on the occasion.

1

2

3

BIRTHDAY GIRL FAN

This fan has small diamonds stamped out. The fan is decorated with Royal Icing piped in dots and zig-zags, and the child's name in the centre.

GOLDEN YEARS FAN

This fan has small holes cut out with pasta and a larger hole in the handle cut out free hand. It is decorated with orange and yellow piped Royal Icing and purchased orange and yellow flowers. The colours can be changed according to the anniversary being celebrated.

WEDDING DAY OR SWEETHEART FAN

This fan has small hearts stamped out. Also, small slits are cut out either free hand or by using a template of the cut out shape. The whole fan is coated in white Royal Icing and allowed to dry. Red Royal Icing is piped on in lines and dots as illustrated.

Magic Lanterns

EASTER LANTERN

> **YOU WILL NEED**
> Golden Gingerbread dough
> (see page 45)
> Hard-boiled sweets, together
> with mimosa, angelica, silver balls
> and "Smarties" (as needed)
> Royal Icing "Cement"
> (see page 48)
> Royal Icing of piping consistency
> (see page 48)
> Food colourings
> 30-cm/12-in cake board
> 5-cm/2-in candle in holder

— METHOD —

1 Cut out an oblong template measuring 7.5 cm/3 in × 15 cm/6 in. This is one side of the lantern. Roll out the gingerbread dough on non-stick paper and lightly mark out 6 oblongs. Use cutters or templates to cut out a cross from the area within the oblong. After this, replace the oblong template over the appropriate area and cut out the sides. This method reduces the amount of distortion.

2 Choose the appropriate colours of boiled sweets and put all of the same colour together (all yellow together, all red together etc) in a plastic bag. Roughly crush with a rolling pin.

3 Bake the gingerbread for 5 minutes. Put a little pile of the crushed sweets into each cut-out and return to the oven for the remaining cooking time instructed under Golden Gingerbread. The sweets will melt, giving a stained glass effect.

1

2

3

4 Remove from the oven and when cool, remove the paper.

5 Using Royal Icing cement, spread a little on the edge of each panel.

6 On a cake board, join the panels together to form a hexagonal shape. Allow to dry, supporting the panels with cans or jars if necessary.

7 When dry, use yellow Royal Icing and a star nozzle, pipe decoratively around the top and bottom, and over the joins of the lantern. Decorate with groups of mimosa balls and angelica leaves placed in the icing on the top edge. Using a plain nozzle, pipe, "Easter Blessings" on three of the panels. Place a lighted candle inside the lantern.

6

4

5

7

CHRISTMAS LANTERN

Follow ingredients and instructions for step 1 of the Easter Lantern.

Using large and small star cutters, stamp out stars from two of the panels and place yellow sweets in cut-outs. Using a Christmas-tree cutter, stamp out trees from two panels and place green sweets in the cut-outs. Using a cutter or template, cut out holly leaves from two panels. Use large pasta for holly berries. Place red and green sweets inside the cut-outs. After baking according to instructions under Golden Gingerbread, assemble the lantern. Using white Royal Icing and a star nozzle, pipe round the top and bottom and over the joins of the lantern. Decorate with silver balls. Using white Royal Icing and a small star nozzle, outline the star cut-out shapes, and, with a plain nozzle, outline the tree cut-out shapes. Using red and green Royal Icing and a plain nozzle, outline the holly and berry cut-outs.

HALLOWE'EN LANTERN

Follow ingredients and instructions for step 1 of the Easter Lantern.

Using Hallowe'en cutters or templates, such as bats, ghosts, cats etc, stamp out shapes from the panels. Use purple, green or orange sweets for the cut-outs. After baking according to instructions under Golden Gingerbread, and the general lantern recipe, assemble the lantern. Using orange-coloured Royal Icing and a star nozzle, pipe decoratively round the top and bottom and over the joins of the lantern. Using green Royal Icing and a plain nozzle, outline the cut-out shapes. Decorate with lilac-coloured "Smarties"

Stained-Glass Biscuits

CHRISTMAS SHAPES

YOU WILL NEED
Golden Gingerbread dough
(see page 45)
Boiled sweets, assorted colours
Ribbon or cord

— METHOD —

Roll out the gingerbread dough. Cut into shapes such as stars, hearts, flowers etc. Cut out the centres of the biscuits, using a similar-shaped smaller cutter, or a plain round cutter.

Make a hole in the top of the biscuit with a skewer. Bake on non-stick paper for four minutes. Add a boiled sweet to the centres and bake for the remaining time as instructed under Golden Gingerbread. When cooked, put the skewer in the holes to open them up. When cold, peel off the non-stick paper. Thread cotton, thin cord or ribbon through the holes and hang the biscuits from the Christmas tree.

EASTER WINDOWS

Follow ingredients for Christmas shapes. Make a template of an arched window as shown. Roll out the gingerbread dough on non-stick paper. Using the template, cut out the window. Make a hole at the top of the gingerbread for hanging. Bake the gingerbread for 5 minutes. Put small piles of different coloured sweets next to one another in the window space. Bake for remaining time as instructed under Golden Gingerbread, during which the coloured sweets will melt and merge together. Allow to become cold before removing from the paper. Thread a cord or ribbon through the hole and hang in a window so the light can shine through.

As an alternative, a very simple window can be made by cutting out an oblong shape and using small aspic cutters to stamp out the centre. Put a different-coloured sweet in each space. Bake as instructed under the Stained Glass Easter Window.

Swedish Christmas Shapes

YOU WILL NEED
Golden Gingerbread dough
(see page 45)
Thin ribbon or thread

— METHOD —

1 Roll out sausages about 25–50 mm/⅛–¼ in in diameter. Try to get the sausages as uniform as possible.

2 When curling the sausages, lie them flat and curl from the outside towards the centre. There are some ideas for you to try on page 67.

1

2

HEART

Bend the sausage in the middle and curl the dough in towards the centre to make a heart shape.

HEART MOTIF

Make 4 small hearts with curled ends and join them together with the pointed ends towards the centre.

SCROLL

Take one sausage and curl each end towards the centre, but do not allow them to touch. Do the same with a second sausage. Join them back to back.

SCROLL TRIANGLE

Simply make three scrolls and join them together in a triangle.

STAR

Make five sausages. Shape each one into an "S" shape that is bigger one end than the other. Make them into a star shape by putting all the small ends of the "S's" towards the centre. Make holes in the shapes using a skewer or a piece of macaroni. Bake as directed under Golden Gingerbread. When cold, thread ribbon or cotton through the shapes and hang as decorations.

Bazaar Bakes

TEDDIES ON A STICK

YOU WILL NEED
Golden Gingerbread dough,
1 batch of light-coloured and 1
batch of dark-coloured
(see page 45)
Wooden lolly sticks
Chocolate dots
Assorted sweets
Glacé Icing (see page 48)
Royal Icing (see page 48),
optional
Shoelace liquorice: black, red,
green, etc

— **METHOD** —

1 Cut out rounds approximately 6 cm/2½ in from the light and dark gingerbread dough. Insert a lolly stick into the base of each biscuit. Cut out two 2.5-cm/1-in rounds for each biscuit. Use light gingerbread rounds with a

dark gingerbread face and vice versa. Place one round on for the nose. Cut the other round in half and use for the ears.

2 Place chocolate dots on the face for the eyes and mouth. Mark the nose with a knife. Bake as instructed under Golden Gingerbread.

1

GINGERBREAD LOLLIES

Follow ingredients for Teddies on a Stick. With round or fluted cutters, carefully cut out the gingerbread dough. Insert a lolly stick into each biscuit. Bake as instructed under Golden Gingerbread.

When cold, stick sweets on the biscuits with Glacé Icing. If liked, pipe "EAT ME", or "YUM YUM" in the centre of each biscuit with Royal Icing.

EDIBLE NECKLACES

Follow ingredients for Teddies on a Stick. Roll out the gingerbread and cut out small shapes such as circles, squares, hearts and diamonds. With a skewer or a piece of macaroni, make a hole at the top. Bake as instructed under Golden Gingerbread.

When cold, decorate with jewel-like sweets, such as fruit gums, boiled sweets, silver balls, etc. Thread liquorice through the top hole.

Teddy Garlands

TEDDY 4TH OF JULY GARLAND

YOU WILL NEED
Golden Gingerbread dough,
(see page 45)
Purchased fondant icing
Paste food colourings
Royal Icing (see page 48)
Popcorn
Thin ribbon or cord
Small cocktail American flags

— **METHOD** —

1 Either use a teddy cutter or make a template (see page 93). Roll out the gingerbread dough and cut out the Teddies.

2 Make two slits on the body at the base of the arms.

3 Bake as instructed under Golden Gingerbread. Cool.

4 Using the cutter or your template, draw a template for Teddy's top and pants.

5 Colour a little of the purchased fondant icing with red food colouring. Roll out and, using the template, carefully cut out a top for each Teddy.

6 Colour a little fondant icing with blue food colouring. Roll out and using the template, cut out pants for each Teddy.

70

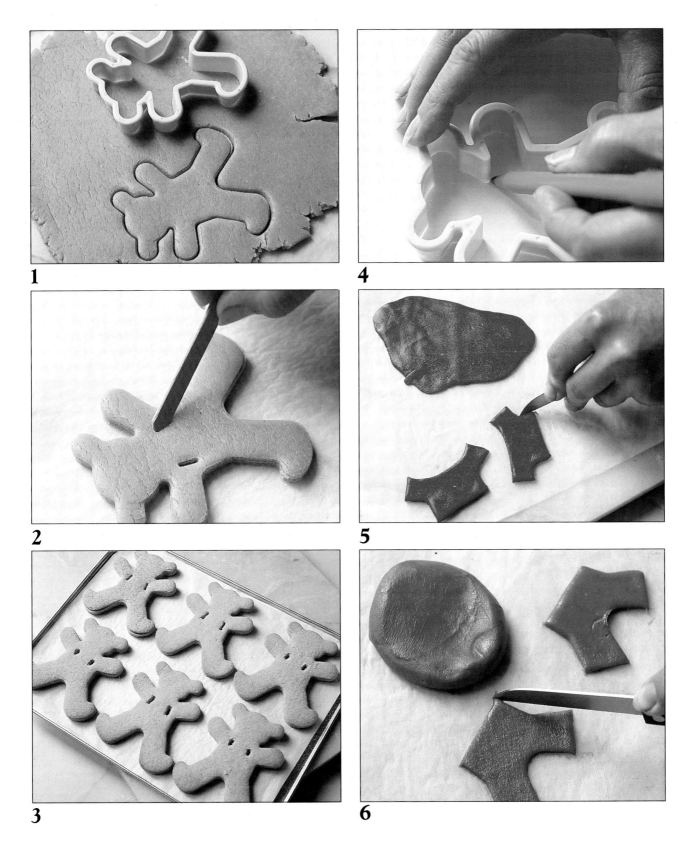

1

2

3

4

5

6

7

8

9

7 Using a little icing glue, stick the clothes onto the Teddies. Make slits in the icing to correspond with the slits in the body. Using white Royal Icing and a small plain nozzle, carefully pipe stripes onto the pants and a bow tie at the neck.

8 Using brown Royal Icing, pipe features onto the faces.

9 Take a long piece of thin ribbon or thread. Tie a knot at one end.

10 Using a large needle, push the thread through the slits in the Teddies' bodies so that the thread lies across the chest.

Then thread on some popcorn. Continue in this way until the desired length is reached. If you are using rib-bon which will not thread through the popcorn, then stick the popcorn on with icing after the Teddies have been threaded on. Finally, stick the flags onto the hands with Royal Icing. Carefully lift the teddy and hang as required.

TEDDY HALLOWE'EN GARLAND

Follow ingredients for Teddy 4th of July Garland. Roll out the gingerbread and cut slits in the body at the base of the arms. Bake as instructed under Golden Gingerbread, and cool. For **Witch Teddy**, colour some fondant icing with black food colouring. Cut out dresses and hats and stick on with Royal Icing. Make slits in the icing to correspond with the body slits. Using Royal Icing tinted green and a plain nozzle, pipe on the witch's hair. To make a **Ghost Teddy**, roll out some white fondant icing and cut out roughly to make a ghost shape as shown. Stick onto a Teddy with Royal Icing. Make slits. Using black food colouring, paint on the ghost's eyes. To make a **Pumpkin Teddy**, colour some fondant icing orange. Roll out and cut out pumpkin shapes. Mark on lines with a knife. Stick the pumpkins onto the Teddies with Royal Icing. Using brown Royal Icing, pipe eyes, nose and mouth on each Teddy. Thread on ribbon or cord with popcorn, as described above.

Gift Tags and Place Names

YOU WILL NEED
Golden Gingerbread dough,
(see page 45)
Dark-coloured Golden
Gingerbread dough (see page 45)
Royal Icing (see page 48)
Edible food colourings
Ribbon or cord

— METHOD —

1 Make a template of the required size, in the shape of a luggage label or gift tag. Roll out the Golden Gingerbread dough and cut out the labels or tags.

2 Make a hole in the pointed end with a skewer or a piece of macaroni. Bake as instructed under Golden Gingerbread.

3 Another version is to roll out and cut out the labels from the light and dark Golden Gingerbread. Using a small cutter, cut out a motif from the centre of each label. Swap the motifs and place a dark one in a light gingerbread label and vice versa. Make a hole in the label.

4 Bake as instructed under Golden Gingerbread dough.

5 When cool, pipe the names and messages as desired, using Royal Icing coloured to your choice and a plain nozzle. There are numerous ways to decorate the labels and tags, so have fun experimenting. When dry, insert a ribbon or ribbon cord through the hole (if applicable) and use as desired.

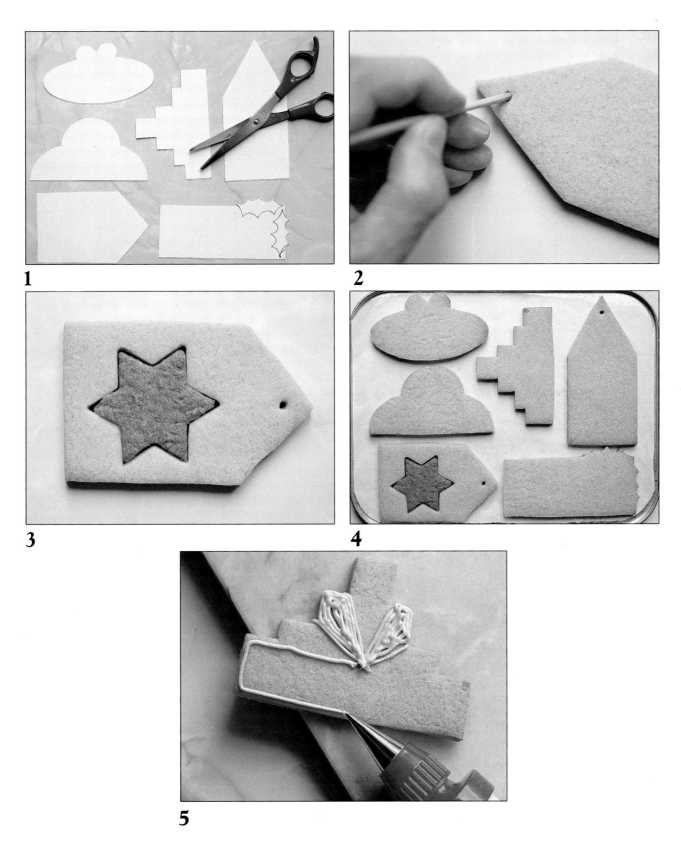

1

2

3

4

5

Mobiles

EASTER MOBILE

YOU WILL NEED
Golden Gingerbread dough,
(see page 45)
Royal Icing (see page 48)
Marshmallows
Glacé Icing (see page 48)
Thin wooden dowels
Thread

— METHOD —

1 Either use cutters or hand-drawn templates to make a gingerbread bunny and eggs of different sizes.

2 Make a hole in the top of the shapes with a skewer or a piece of macaroni. Bake as instructed under Golden Gingerbread.

1

2

3 When cold, outline the rabbits with white Royal Icing, using a plain nozzle. Using a little extra icing, stick a white marshmallow onto each bunny to represent the tail.

4 Decorate the eggs in various patterns using Royal Icing tinted in shades of lilac, yellow, orange, green and pale blue. Some ideas are illustrated.

5 To make the mobile, arrange the eggs and bunnies on a table. Attach threads to each one. Tie on to thin wooden dowels.

6 Adjust the balance by sliding the threads along the dowels. Find the point of balance on each dowel before attaching the next one. Hang where there is space for the mobile to move.

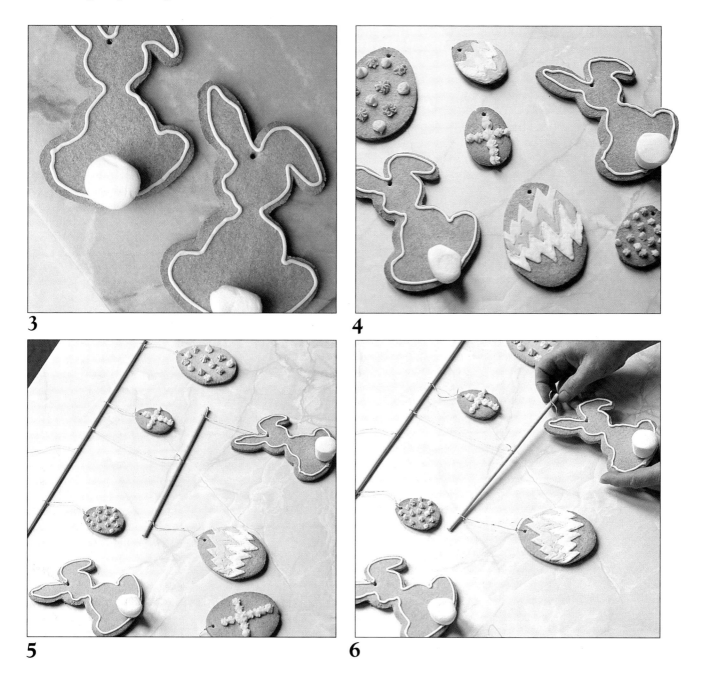

3

4

5

6

MOTHER'S DAY MOBILE

Follow ingredients for Easter Mobile. Using cutters or templates, cut out gingerbread flowers and parcels. Make holes in the top with a skewer or macaroni. Bake as instructed under Golden Gingerbread. When cold, ice with coloured Royal Icing, as illustrated.

Stars

STAR BURSTS

YOU WILL NEED
Golden Gingerbread dough,
(see page 45)
Royal Icing (see page 48)
Edible food colourings

— METHOD —

1 Roll out the gingerbread dough and carefully cut out different sizes of star shapes, using cutters or templates. Bake as instructed under Golden Gingerbread.

2 Make up some Royal Icing of coating consistency. Pour into several small containers and colour with food colouring.

3 Spread icing over the stars.

4 With a teaspoon, drip tinted icings carefully onto the coating before it sets.

5 With a toothpick, draw connecting lines between the drops, to form random patterns.

1

2

3

4

5

STAR TREE

YOU WILL NEED
Construction Gingerbread
(see page 44)
Royal Icing (see page 48)
Green food colouring
Red sweets
Small red candle

— METHOD —

1 For this you will need a set of six graded star cutters. Or cut out some graded star templates of your own. Roll the dough out thickly and carefully cut out about 3 or 4 biscuits of each size star. Bake as instructed under Construction Gingerbread.

2 When cold, ice the biscuits with green Royal Icing of coating consistency. Allow to dry thoroughly.

3 Build the tree on a cake board or suitable serving dish. Start with the largest star and secure it with a dab of Royal Icing. Place a second star on top, securing with icing and placing so that the points of the star are at the indentations of the first star.

4 Continue stacking the stars, decreasing in size and changing the angle of each as you build. Finally, place a small red candle on top. Decorate with small red sweets.

1

2

3

4

Hearts

LARGE VALENTINE HEART

— METHOD —

1 Using Golden Gingerbread dough, and either cutters or templates, cut out very large heart shapes (about 15–25 cm/6–10 in in size). Bake as instructed under Golden Gingerbread. Cool. When cold, cover in melted chocolate or cake covering.

2 Using Royal Icing and a star nozzle, pipe a decoration round the edge, and stick on the sweets. Using Royal Icing and a plain nozzle, pipe a message in the centre.

1

2

HEART BOX

Follow ingredients for the Large Valentine Heart. Using a small (approx 18-cm/7-in) round- or heart-shaped sandwich tin, grease the *outside* and place upside down on a baking tray. Roll out some Construction Gingerbread dough on non-stick paper. Using the non-stick paper, lift the gingerbread and turn it onto the tin. Fold the dough over the tin. Peel off the paper and gently push out any air bubbles from the dough. Trim the edge of the ginger-bread. Bake for about 12–15 minutes. Remove from the oven and trim the bottom edge of the case. Allow to cool for 5 minutes before carefully removing the case from the tin. Roll out the rest of the Construction Gingerbread. Use the tin as a guide and cut out a lid which is slightly larger than the tin. Using the Golden Gingerbread, cut out heart shapes and arrange on the lid as decoration. Bake as instructed under Construction Gingerbread. When cold, decorate with Royal Icing, as shown. Use the box as a container for biscuits.

HEART GARLAND

Follow ingredients for the Large Valentine Heart. Using light and dark Golden Ginger-bread dough, cut out several hearts in different sizes. On non-stick paper, arrange the hearts in a circle, overlapping them so that they join together. Bake as instructed under Golden Gingerbread. Decorate with piped Royal Icing, if desired.

Garlands

THANKSGIVING GARLAND

YOU WILL NEED
Construction Gingerbread dough
(see page 44)
Ribbon
Glacé or Royal Icing
(see page 46), optional
Food colourings

— METHOD —

1 Roll out Construction Gingerbread on non-stick paper.

2 Using a plate or a template, cut out a circle (about 23 cm/9 in).

1

2

3

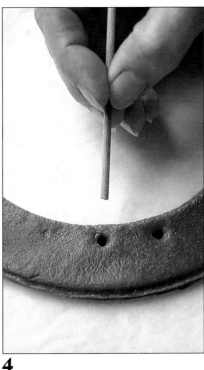

4

3 Using a smaller plate or template, cut another circle from the centre of the first one. The rim of the garland should be about 4–5-cm/1½–2-in wide.

4 Using large macaroni, a piping tube or apple corer, cut out holes for ribbon.

5

6

5 Using real leaves as models, make the templates.

6 Cut out a variety of different leaf shapes and arrange on the garland. Bake as instructed under Construction Gingerbread. When cold, thread ribbon through the holes and tie in a bow. Make some Glacé or Royal Icing and tint in Autumn leaf colours. Using a brush, paint the icing on the leaves.

CHRISTMAS GARLAND

Follow steps 1–4 as for the Thanksgiving Garland. Make two small holes at the top for a ribbon. Cut out holly leaf shapes and roll gingerbread holly berries. Arrange attractively on the garland. Make small letters using the "sausage" method as described in Children's Corner (see page 53) and put the words "Merry Xmas" on the garland. Bake as instructed under Construction Gingerbread. When cold, tie a red ribbon at the top.

HAPPY BIRTHDAY GARLAND

Follow steps 1–4 as for the Thanksgiving Garland. Cut out leaves and mark the veins with a knife. To make tassel flowers, roll out offcuts of the gingerbread, and cut along their length. Roll up and you have a tassel which can be gently opened out. Arrange the tassel flowers on the garland. Make either "sausage" or "knobbly" letters – or use letter cutters – to spell out a name or "HAPPY BIRTHDAY". Bake as instructed under Construction Gingerbread. When cold, thread a pink ribbon through the holes and tie a ribbon at the top.

Hansel and Gretel House

YOU WILL NEED

Construction Gingerbread
(see page 44)

Boiled sweets (for windows)

Royal Icing "Cement"
(see page 48)

Royal Icing (see page 48)

Large cake board

Roof tiles – suggestions include
chocolate-covered finger biscuits,
marshmallow twists, or candy canes
for roof ridge; flat biscuits,
chocolate mints or chocolate
flakes, for the roof itself

Wall decorations – suggestions
include candy canes, jelly
diamonds, "Smarties", fruit gums,
fruit pastilles, jelly beans, liquorice
all-sorts, dolly mixtures etc.

— METHOD —

1 Make templates out of thin card (see pages 94 and 95). You should have the following:

- 1 front with cut-out window and cut-out doors, which are reserved and cooked separately.
- 1 back, plain with no cut-outs.
- 1 side, with 3 arched windows cut-out.
- 1 side, plain with no cut-outs.
- 1 side of roof, plain with no cut-out.
- 1 side of roof with cut-out for gable window.
- Gable window, 4 pieces – frame.
- 2 sides and roof.
- Chimney stack, 4 pieces.

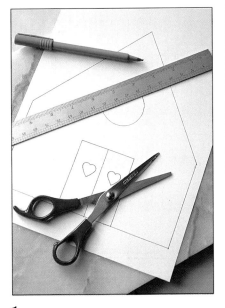

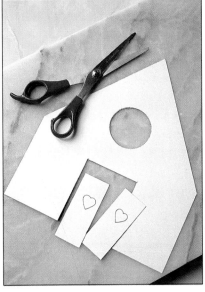

1

2 For the large pieces, roll out the gingerbread to 4mm/¼ in thickness on non-stick paper. Cut out shapes and trim off the excess dough. This can be re-rolled for further shapes. Bake according to instructions for Construction Gingerbread.

2

3 Halfway through the cooking time, place a coloured boiled sweet in each window. Large windows may need 2 sweets.

3

4 For the chimney stack and gable windows, roll the dough out to 2mm/ ⅛ in thick on non-stick paper. Bake as instructed. Put boiled sweets in the gable window cut-outs, halfway through cooking time. If any pieces become misshapen during cooking, put the appropriate template on top and trim the edges while still warm. Leave the pieces to cool completely (overnight is best) before assembling.

4

5 Assemble the house on a large cake board. Using Royal Icing "Cement", apply icing to the bottom edge and the side edge of the back piece. Position the back and the side at right angles on the cake board.

6 Join the front and the other side together, as above. Using Royal Icing "Cement" on the remaining edges, join the front and side to the back and side already on the board. Prop the walls upright with cans or jars and leave until set.

7 Assemble the chimney stack and leave to dry on non-stick paper.

8 Spread the "Cement" icing on the underside edges of the roof pieces and place in position on the top of house. Support in position until dry.

5

7

6

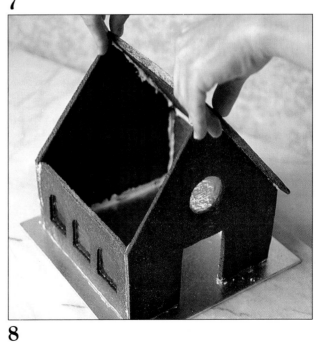

8

9 Using Royal Icing "Cement", stick the two side panels and the front panel of gable window in the space in the roof, as shown. When set, stick the roof onto the gable window with Royal Icing "Cement".

10 Stick the chimney on the opposite side of the roof to the gable window.

11 Stick the doors in "open" position in the doorway. Fill any gaps with Royal Icing "Cement".

12 Now decorate the house according to your fancy. Using Royal Icing "Cement", stick the chosen roof "tiles" on the roof. This is just a guide. Then, using Royal Icing "Cement", stick sweets lavishly on the walls of the house. Using Royal Icing, (or watered down "Cement"), pipe icicles hanging from the roof eaves, window sills etc.

9

11

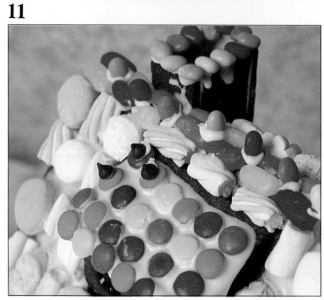

12

10

13

13 Surround the house with Royal Icing snow and, if liked, a fence can be stuck around, using a suitable sweet such as a "Curly Wurly", or even marshmallows or pink wafer biscuits. If liked, gingerbread trees and figures can be placed outside the house as described in Star Tree project (see page 80).

Templates

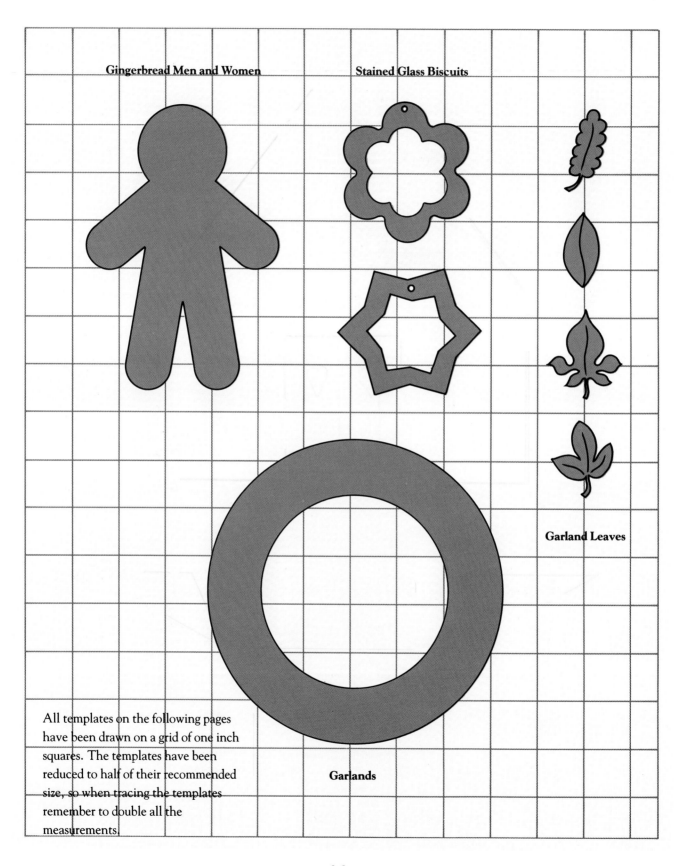

Gingerbread Men and Women

Stained Glass Biscuits

Garland Leaves

Garlands

All templates on the following pages have been drawn on a grid of one inch squares. The templates have been reduced to half of their recommended size, so when tracing the templates remember to double all the measurements.

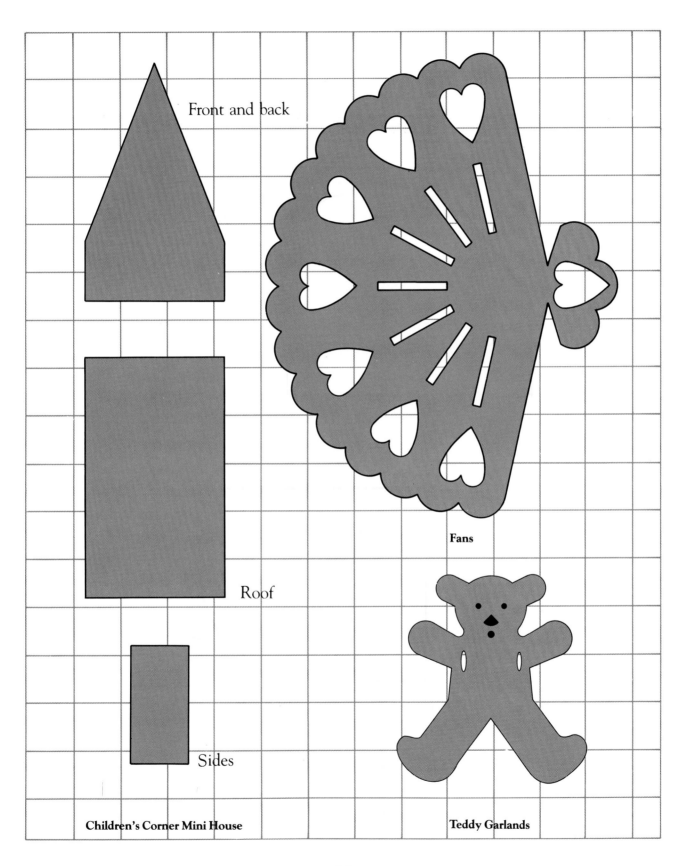

Front and back

Fans

Roof

Sides

Children's Corner Mini House

Teddy Garlands

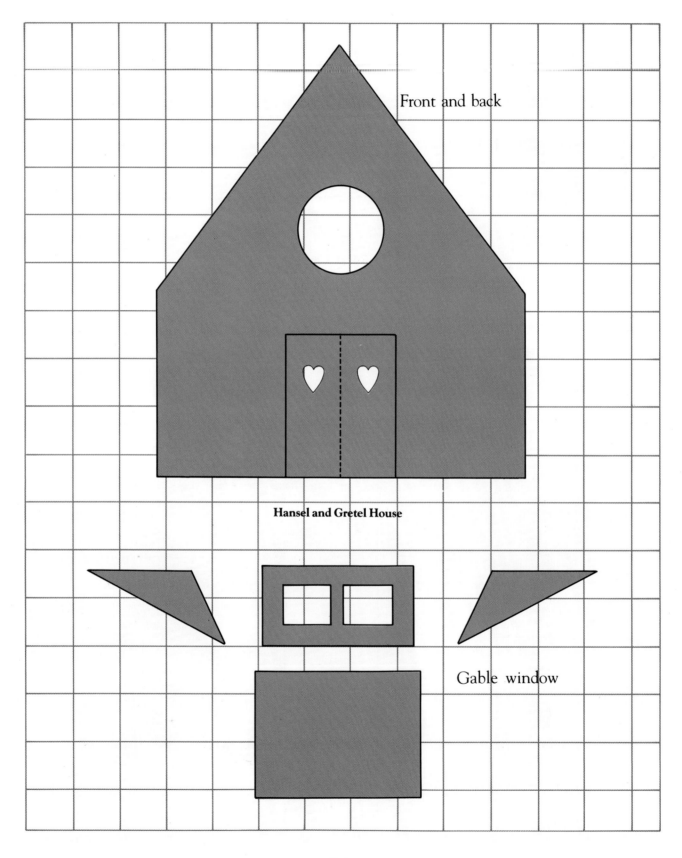

Front and back

Hansel and Gretel House

Gable window

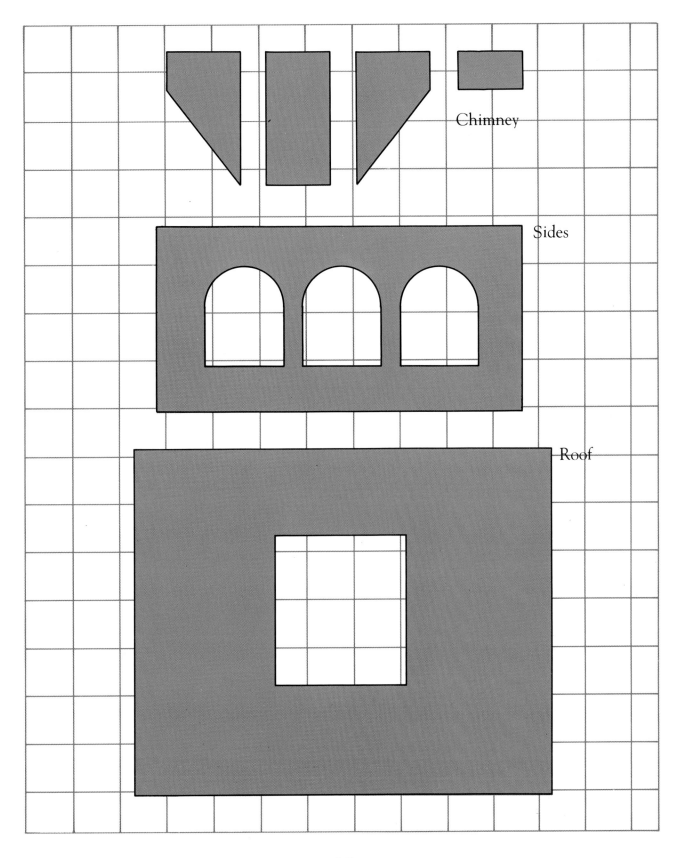

Chimney

Sides

Roof

Index